Praise for Penelope Leach's

WHEN PARENTS PART

"What a splendid book! Read it to save your children from marital mess and divorce-induced grief."　　—Oliver James, author of
Affluenza and *How to Develop Emotional Health*

"With typical insight and without passing judgment, Penelope Leach addresses a subject that is, for many, an inescapable aspect of modern parenting. Separation may be unavoidable, but separating badly doesn't have to be: Leach shows us how to go about it in the best possible way, for children—and adults."
—Justine Roberts, CEO of Mumsnet

"A must-read for any professional who deals with or encounters divorced parents and their children. . . . Though broad and thorough in coverage, it is remarkably easy to read. . . . The margin boxes with snippets of real family situations add a particularly human touch. . . . Essential aspects of custody and collaboration are handled smoothly in this incredible one-source volume. It is such a worthy read."
—John R. Lutzker, Ph.D.,
director of the Mark Chaffin Center for Healthy Development

"When it comes to the more challenging aspects of giving parenting advice on child development, I have always felt that Penelope Leach is a safe pair of hands. Here Leach brings her direct yet sensitive approach to the difficult subject of parental separation and its potential effect on children's well-being. . . . Leach's extensive experience of advising parents is at its most valuable here."
—Richard Bowlby, president of the Centre for Child Mental Health

Penelope Leach

WHEN PARENTS PART

Penelope Leach is a research psychologist, a fellow of the British Psychological Society, a visiting professor at the University of Winchester, and a senior research fellow at Birkbeck, University of London, and at the Tavistock and Portman NHS Foundation Trust. She has been president of the National Childminding Association, vice president of the Health Visitors Association, and president and chair of the Child Development Society. She has also been a consulting editor at *Child* magazine; a member of the Professional Advisory Council of the American Institute for Child, Adolescent, and Family Studies; and a member of the curricula board of *Sesame Street*.

Also by Penelope Leach

Child Care Today

The Essential First Year

Children First

The First Six Months

Your Growing Child

Your Baby & Child

Babyhood

WHEN
PARENTS
PART

WHEN
PARENTS
PART

**How Mothers and Fathers
Can Help Their Children Deal with
Separation and Divorce**

Penelope Leach

Vintage Books
A Division of Penguin Random House LLC
New York

FIRST VINTAGE BOOKS EDITION, OCTOBER 2016

Copyright © 2014, 2015 by Penelope Leach

The Library of Congress has cataloged the Knopf edition as follows:
Leach, Penelope.
[Family breakdown]
When parents part : how mothers and fathers can help their children deal with separation and divorce / Penelope Leach.
pages cm
Originally published in Great Britain in 2014 as: Family breakdown : helping children hang on to both their parents.
Includes bibliographical references and index.
1. Divorce.   2. Children of divorced parents.   3. Parenting.   I. Title.
HO814.L425 2015   306.89—dc23   2015009350

Vintage Books Trade Paperback ISBN: 978-1-101-87219-2
eBook ISBN: 978-1-101-87405-9

Author photograph © Alex Gregory
Book design by Cassandra J. Pappas

www.vintagebooks.com

Printed in the United States of America
10   9   8   7   6   5   4   3   2   1

*My thanks to all the children, young people, and adults
who have talked to me about their parents parting.
They talked because they wanted children to be heard.
We are listening.*

Contents

Introduction

In the United States (and indeed across most of the Western world) family breakdown is at epidemic levels in every part of society. If divorce, especially divorce involving children, was a physical disease, it would undoubtedly attract government funding for emergency research to develop a vaccine and provide a mass immunization and treatment program. But accustomed as we are to ignoring parental separation and taking divorces for granted, comparison with a national medical emergency sounds almost fanciful. It is not so, though. Family breakdown is the elephant in the room in more than half the homes in the United States, and it's time we paid it attention.

If you are separating, divorcing, or seriously considering doing so, you're not alone; you're not even in a minority. So many parents separate, whether from formal marriages, from civil partnerships, or from cohabitation, that in the English-speaking world today only about half of all children celebrate their sixteenth birthdays with their biological parents still living together.

Tradition has it that marriage should last "until death do us part," but in the modern Western world, where an average lifetime exceeds seventy years, it's often divorce rather than death that ends marriages. According to the National Center for Health Statistics Reports, between 2006 and 2010 the probability of a first marriage in the United States lasting at least ten years was

DIVORCE STATISTICS

In 2012 widely accepted estimates put the lifelong probability of a U.S. marriage ending in divorce at 40–50 percent.

In 2002 (the latest survey data available) the percentages of married individuals who reached their fifth, tenth, and fifteenth anniversaries were 82 percent, 65 percent, and 52 percent, respectively.

The longer a marriage lasts, the less the likelihood of it ending in divorce and the greater the probability of it being ended by death.

The percentages of married individuals reaching their twenty-fifth, thirty-fifth, and fiftieth anniversaries were 33 percent, 20 percent, and 5 percent, respectively.

Analyses and predictions are complex because many factors affect them:

- Previous marriage: individuals who have not been married before are less likely to divorce.
- Higher education and age at marriage also correspond to longer-lasting marriages. For example, of college graduates marrying in the 1980s, 81 percent of those who wed when over twenty-six years of age were still married twenty years later, whereas only 65 percent of those who married under the age of twenty-six were still married twenty years later. In 2009, 2.9 percent of adults aged thirty-five to thirty-nine without a college degree were divorced compared with only 1.6 percent of adults in the same age range who had a college education.
- Wealth and sexual satisfaction have been shown to correlate negatively with divorce rates in the United States. Richer and more sexually satisfied individuals are less likely to divorce.
- A 2008 study on behalf of the Education Resources Information Center showed higher divorce rates among interracial than for same-race

68 percent for women and 70 percent for men. The probability of a first marriage surviving to twenty years was 52 percent for women and 56 percent for men. The state with the highest reported divorce rate was Nevada (6.4 per 1,000) and the lowest was the District of Columbia (1.7 per 1,000), closely followed by Massachusetts and Pennsylvania (2.2 and 2.5 per 1,000).

couples. Marriages between white females and nonwhite males were the most vulnerable.

■ Divorce is less likely if couples share a religious faith. In a 1993 study in the United States, couples who were each members of two mainline Protestant religions had a 20 percent chance of being divorced in five years, whereas a couple consisting of a Catholic and an Evangelical individual had a 33 percent chance, and a couple in which one partner was Jewish and the other was Christian had a 40 percent chance. By 2001, marriages between people who regularly attended a religious service of any faith and those who attended infrequently were three times more likely to end in divorce.

In 2013 *The Huffington Post* analyzed and published the results of a range of contemporary divorce-related studies:

■ The overall numbers of divorced females are rising. The number of women divorced or divorcing has reached 15 percent.

■ Women who had been raped or who had lost their virginity before the age of eighteen were more likely to divorce.

■ A couple's relative (not absolute) alcohol consumption has a bearing on the stability of marriage. Couples in which one spouse drinks substantially more than the other are significantly more likely to divorce.

■ A daily commute of forty-five minutes or more each way significantly increased the likelihood of a couple separating.

Source: Copen et al. 2012; http://www.huffingtonpost.com/
news/us-divorce-rate/, 2013 statistics

The social organization of the United States, and of most societies in the West, is still based on families interlinked through marriage, although the statistics above make it clear that maintaining a good marriage against the social and sexual pressures and long duration of modern life is very difficult indeed. The effects of family breakdown, parental separation, and divorce on children are profound and permanent. They are not only affected by family breakdown at the time but also during the remaining years of their childhood and, to a greater or lesser extent, throughout their lives. And it is not only the children and parents who suffer when a family breaks down: there's a ripple effect that spreads up to the grandparent generation and down to the next generation—to children who are still in the future, including the children of today's children, whose parenting will be affected by their parents' experiences. And there are horizontal effects, too, on the wider family (sisters, brothers, aunts, uncles, and cousins), on the community of which the family is part, and, ultimately, on the whole of society. So the divorce epidemic means that the traditional and accepted foundations of civil society are crumbling and thus far they are not being replaced.

The only alternative that has emerged into social acceptability is cohabitation. More than a third of American children under sixteen will spend some time in a cohabiting household. There is research—and political comment—suggesting that cohabitation is less stable and lasting than marriage. It is also suggested that having cohabiting rather than married parents is a disadvantage to children. In the United Kingdom in 2007, for example, seventeen-year-olds whose parents were cohabiting were less likely to remain in school than those whose natural (not step-) parents were married. In the United States, black and Hispanic children are over-represented in cohabiting families compared with white children and are thought to be at greater risk of instability. However, cohabitation is not always very different from marriage and often precedes it. Reported statistics often fail to distinguish between children who were planned within and born to cohabiting parents and unplanned children born to single mothers who later lived with someone who was not the father.

When a marriage ends, so does the married couple's relationship, but when cohabitation ends, it often becomes marriage. Getting married after a long period of cohabitation and the birth of children is increasingly common. For some couples, such a wedding is a ceremonial, public celebration of the family they

MARRIAGE, COHABITATION, AND BIRTH STATISTICS

The number of couples who marry is falling. In the United States in 1970, 71.7 percent of adults were married; in 2000 the comparable figure was 59.5 percent.

Couples living together, including same-sex couples linked in civil partnerships, are the fastest-growing family unit in the West. From 1987 to 2002, the percentage of American women in their thirties who had ever cohabited doubled, from 30 percent to 61 percent. Approximately half of all the men and women who married in the United States after 1995 were previously living together. European statistics are similar: numbers of cohabiting couples in the United Kingdom rose by 65 percent between 1996 and 2006, from 1.4 million to 2.3 million.

The number of babies born to mothers who were not married naturally rises with the rise in cohabitation. In 2012, 47 percent of babies born in England and Wales had parents who were not married.

In 2008, 40.6 percent of babies born in the United States had cohabiting parents. Overall, 15 percent of those children experienced the end of their parents' unions by age one, half by age five, and two-thirds by age ten.

The most recent figures on both sides of the Atlantic predict that by 2016 more than half of all babies will be born "out of wedlock."

Source: P. Smock and N. Manning in DiFonzo 2011;
Office for National Statistics 2014

have made; children—and sometimes stepchildren, too—often take part. For older couples, the main reasons for an eventual marriage ceremony may be legal and financial, perhaps having to do with pensions and inheritance.

The dramatic fall in the number of couples who marry is largely due to changes in attitudes toward sex, marriage, and having children, but also toward the practical changes brought about by increasingly available and efficient contraception and by the rise in women's incomes. In the 1960s and 1970s getting married was an intrinsic part of being recognized as an adult: it meant being able to have sex, to live together, and to have children. This is no longer the case. People do all these things without first being married. Not everyone approves of the change, however.

National poll results from the Pew Research Center's Social and Demographic Trends project (2010) and from the 2009 American Community Survey showed strong support for marriage as the exclusive moral framework for sexual relationships and childbearing: 45 percent of respondents thought it morally wrong to have a baby outside of marriage, and 40 percent thought that sexual relationships between unmarried women and men were morally wrong; 30 percent also thought that divorce was morally wrong, irrespective of the circumstances. However, in a study of the first wave of millennials to become parents, a team from Johns Hopkins University found that 64 percent of mothers gave birth at least once out of wedlock. Almost half had all their children without ever exchanging vows (Weissmann 2014).

It is clear that whether they live together with or without marriage and whether or not they have children, most adults seek committed partnerships. However, it is also clear that there are many individuals who cannot remain content for their whole adult life living with one partner in a monogamous relationship, which is a basic expectation of marriage or permanent partnership. There has to be a way that individuals can escape or move on, with as little damage as possible to themselves and to their nuclear and extended families. People can escape by separating and increasingly they move on through divorce, but the damage that is done, especially to children, is sometimes appalling and often far greater than it need be.

How can parental separation and divorce be managed better from children's point of view? This is a question of national importance, and any real chance of finding answers depends on information and dispassionate debate based on hard facts and careful research rather than on prejudice and moralizing. Relevant research exists; data are out there, but they are often hard to find or interpret, and they are sometimes unwelcome.

This book surveys the entire canvas of family breakdown in

depth. It looks at the multifaceted problem of parental separation and divorce from every angle: emotional, scientific, psychological, practical, and legal. It intermixes irrefutable hard facts,
up-to-the-minute statistical details, changes in legal practice,
and scientific research, including highly relevant recent findings
from research into the neuroscience of child development. And
it interweaves throughout the voices of children and of parents,
bringing to life what all this actually means to families and high-
lighting what could be done better.

Until two centuries ago, bad marriages on both sides of
the Atlantic had to be endured for a lifetime. Up to 1858 fewer
than three hundred divorces had been granted in England and
Wales. In the United States, however, beginning in the 1800s,
early feminists such as Elizabeth Cady Stanton crusaded for
the right to divorce, and "by 1880 one in 16 U.S. marriages was
ending in divorce, already the highest rate in the world" (Clark
1996). According to a report by the New England Divorce Reform
League released in 1889, "divorce had risen dramatically in the
United States; from 9,937 in 1867 to 25,535 in 1886—more than a
150 percent increase" (Jost and Robinson 1991). Now separation
and divorce, new partnerships, remarriages, and step-parenting
are such big parts of life for many people, and so familiar to
everyone, that it's difficult to believe that they are little more
than a century old.

Because being trapped in an unhappy marriage or forced to
go through socially unacceptable divorce proceedings produced
dreadful hardship for so many in the past, we should welcome
the fact that divorce is now a well-established part of civil society
via family law. However, it is one thing to welcome the existence
of legal divorce, and perhaps press for it to be increasingly accessible, and quite another to welcome the actual process and its
potential consequences.

In the twenty-first century, divorce at its worst can still be bitterly antagonistic, and even at its best it is very seldom pain-free,
even for the partner who sought the separation. Being granted
that decree may feel like liberation from a relationship that has

gone sour or worse; if there is a new partner waiting in the wings, it may even feel like the beginning of a new, exciting, and romantic life. But even if the divorce works out well for one partner, it will almost certainly be bad—emotionally and financially—for the other. And for a couple who have children, trying to spread the love, the energy, and the income that used to power one household between the two that now exist is horribly stressful, and so is the fact that however good the separation may be for both adults, it will quite certainly be bad for their children.

Does that serious, even grim, message have a subtext suggesting that parents should stay together "for the sake of the children"? No, it does not. The more couples who can be helped to improve their relationship to a point where they stay together because they want to, the better. But an unhappy partnership is unlikely to make for good parenting or happy children. And whether outsiders can understand the reasons for the breakup or not, parents (as opposed to childless couples) seldom separate or divorce lightly. Sometimes it seems as if that is so, as if they

IMPACT OF SEPARATION AND DIVORCE ON ADULT MENTAL AND PHYSICAL HEALTH

In a random sample of 353,492 American adults, those who were separated or divorced had lower scores on the Well-Being Index, which covers emotional and physical health, health behaviors, life evaluation, work environment, and access to basic necessities. The managing editor of the think tank Gallup, Jeffrey Jones, calls these differences "staggering."

Source: Brown and Jones 2012

In register-based data for 304,111 adult Finns, those approaching or experiencing separation or divorce were significantly more likely to use psychotropic medication (especially for depression). Following divorce, there was excess mortality among males (though not females), especially attributable to accidental, violent, or alcohol-related causes.

Source: Metsä-Simola and Martikainen 2013a, 2013b

could have kept the relationship going if they had really tried, but it usually turns out that the immediate and seemingly trivial reason for parting (such as the boredom of the woman quoted below) is the final straw rather than the real cause. Separation is an event in a long process of family breakdown, and when that process is understood, it usually shines a different light on what is best for the children.

The woman's decision here may sound selfish, and announced in this way to her husband and children, it probably seemed like a bolt from the blue. In truth, though, it was a shaft of light out of gray skies. Absence of

> **Mother of three children, aged four, six, and nine**
> "I have a cousin in New Zealand, and she's offered me a job in her own firm. No, my husband isn't coming. Yes, of course I asked him, but he wouldn't dream of leaving his job and pulling up roots. But that's only his problem now, not mine. I've been bored out of my skull for a long time, and this is a new start in a new country for me and the kids, with a job I can make something of for all of us."

love, affection, shared goals, or even everyday tolerance between parents leaves a chilly gap in children's lives whether they are eight months old, eight years old, or eighteen years old. The icy silence of that kind of long-term dissatisfaction isn't as easily recognized as open parental irritation, depression, or the sexual unfaithfulness, arguments, enmity, and especially violence that poison many children's growing up. But if the long-term relationship between parents has gradually become joyless or intolerable to one or both of them, it will not be a good environment for their children.

We have to accept divorce (and separation) as a safety valve for marriage and cohabitation. Adult society cannot do without one. But the well-being of children who will grow up to form that society in their turn is being put at risk by the way that safety valve is deployed. We can manage separation and divorce better. With children in mind, we should.

As people-who-are-parents, you may divorce or leave each other, but you cannot divorce and should never leave your children. As a family breaks up, the needs of its children should be the adults' priority, not only for the sake of the children's current happiness and well-being but also for the sake of the people they are going to become in the future. It is everyone's good fortune that in this new millennium we know more than ever before about what those needs are.

PART I

When Parents Separate,
What Makes a Difference to Children?

Seeing Children's Points of View

The breakup of a family isn't an event; it's a process and often a very long, slow one. Even if one partner has physically left, swearing that that's it, he'll have to come back. He'll return for his belongings, for more agonizing conversations, arguments, and accusations, and maybe for some unexpected moments of nostalgic regret when the toddler holds up her arms to greet him and the dog licks his hand. The two of them nearly get back together again and he mows the lawn.

This is adult business at its most intense, and with this kind of stuff taking up most of your attention, you won't have much to spare for anybody or anything else, including your children.

But this adult business is very much children's business as well. It may be your marriage that's breaking up, but it's their family. You are losing your husband, wife,

Girl, aged ten
"When she was driving, she just didn't seem to notice the lights changing, so we all yelled, 'Lights!' when we came up to a red one."

Boy, aged eight
"Dad came to see Mom in the morning. Just Mom. Not me. How do I know? Because he was surprised to see me home. He'd actually forgotten vacation had started."

or partner, but they are losing not only the parent who is physically absent but both Daddy and Mommy, because even when you are present, neither of you is the parent they had in the past.

Girl, aged six
"Mostly Mommy doesn't hear me anymore. She just says, 'Mmm.'"

Deciding to separate has committed both of you to confusion in the present and, eventually, to finding new ways of life; your children had no part in the making of that decision and have no choice about what happens next. Your separation will turn your children's lives upside down and inside out. There's nothing you can do to prevent that, but if you recognize what's likely to make things better or worse for each child, then there is a lot you can do to moderate the storm.

Nearly half of U.S. marriages end in divorce. Divorce statistics like this make good shock headlines, but focused as they are on divorce as adult business rather than on family breakdown, they tell us astonishingly little about children. That focus is wrong, both factually and morally. In the last two decades it has become clear that parental separation is very much children's business, and that instead of being involved principally as weapons in marital war, they should be recognized as its victims. Family breakdowns are commonplace, but that does not mean they are trivial—far from it. For children of all ages, from birth into adulthood, having the family split up is always deeply disruptive, usually sad and saddening, and sometimes tragic.

The message that parental separation always makes children unhappy is not one that parents want to hear, so if it is mentioned at all, it is usually only offered to them well diluted with reassurances about children being "resilient" and quickly "getting over it." For children's sakes, though, it is a message that needs to be widely broadcast and swallowed neat. Separating or getting divorced is a bad break for all of you, and you need to face the fact that children are no more likely than you are yourselves to "get over it" in the sense of forgetting about it or it ceasing to be important.

However willing you may be to face up to the impact your separation is likely to have on your children, you may not find it easy to get reliable and relevant information, because official statistics are mostly about divorce only rather than about all separations and are very inadequate sources of information about children. Not every divorce affects a child directly; in the United States about one-third of divorcing or separating couples are childless, and in those in which children are involved, marital problems will have been affecting them long before their parents actually get a decree and a place in the statistics. A great many children are affected by parental separations that never reach the divorce court, either because the marriages broke up without the spouses seeking divorce or because the parental partnerships had no official rubber stamp at the beginning and therefore have none when they end. None of these situations appear in those statistics. Even when statistics are given for divorces in which children are known to be involved, they tell us very little about those children—how many were involved per family or in total; their sexes; their actual ages when divorce was granted or

---

CHILDREN WITH SEPARATED PARENTS: SATISFACTION WITH LIFE

The degree of satisfaction with life of 50,000 children aged thirteen, fourteen, and fifteen with separated parents was compared with the degree of satisfaction of 150,000 children from intact families in thirty-six Western countries.

Children in all post-divorce household types were less satisfied with life than children in intact families:

- Shared custody –.21 (least difference from intact families)
- Mother and stepfather –.33
- Single mother –.28
- Single father –.49
- Father and stepmother –.62 (biggest difference from intact families)

Source: Nielsen et al. 2012

even approximate ages when their parents' marriage began to disintegrate.

Statistics concerned with the proportion of families that are headed by a single parent are a little more child-focused, of course, but their information is not straightforward because they seldom differentiate between families in which the parents have separated and those that have been single-parent from the beginning or in which one parent has died. They do serve to remind us, though, that many separations and divorces mean many single parents. According to the latest U.S. Census, there were 11.7 million single parents in the United States in 2010, of whom 85 percent (9.9 million) were custodial mothers and 15 percent (1.8 million) were custodial fathers. Figures for the United Kingdom are slightly different: of 2 million single parents, 92 percent are custodial mothers and 8 percent are custodial fathers; 1.9 million single parents each have one child under sixteen, 621,000 have two children, and 238,000 have three or more.

In a large majority of single-parent families, the mother is the custodial parent, and it is the father who is absent. It may be the other way around in your case, of course, but if so, you are in a minority and a very small one at that. It is often assumed that it is mothers who end up as single parents primarily because men are more likely than women to walk out on their families or because it is still widely assumed—by separating couples themselves as well as by society and the family courts that represent it—that when parents separate, it is more appropriate for mothers

ESTIMATED PROPORTIONS OF FAMILIES IN ENGLISH-SPEAKING COUNTRIES THAT HAVE ONLY ONE PARENT

Australia: one in six	South Africa: one in three
Canada: one in four	United Kingdom: one in four
New Zealand: one in seven	United States: one in three

Source: Examples from the United Nations Economic Commission for Europe 2014

rather than fathers to take daily charge of the children. However, there are even more basic reasons for the relative scarcity of single-parent men. First, there is a far greater likelihood of early death among males, so if a child has only one living parent, it will probably be his mother. Second, there is as yet no male equivalent to the "unmarried mother," although with the use of donor eggs and surrogacy this may change.

STATISTICS THAT TELL US how many families were without one parent tell us little about the reasons and rarely anything about what is happening now, or will happen in the future, to the children within those families. Indeed, we cannot even be sure what "family" means or whether the way the term is used in one study is the same as the way it is used in another. Most people assume that "family" is about men and women having children together, but not every family is based on heterosexual relationships. A tiny but growing minority of children may be born to or brought up by a homosexual couple, who may be male or female and married, in a civil partnership, or cohabiting. A large majority of children are born to heterosexual couples of course, but with no guarantee that the nuclear family will be stable. For all children, there is almost a fifty-fifty chance that their parents will separate, and if they do, children's subsequent experiences of "family" are likely to be far more complicated than simplistic statistical summaries suggest, because one or both parents are likely to form new partnerships that will have an even higher likelihood of breaking down. The breakdown rate for second marriages in the United States as a whole is 60–67 percent, and for third marriages it is around 74 percent. A parental divorce followed by even one lover per parent and one new spouse each makes four combinations of parent and parent figure, and each new combination may bring the child new grandparent, aunt or uncle, and cousin figures, as well as stepsiblings or half-siblings, some of whom may be peers while others may be quasi adults.

WHEN YOU ARE THINKING about what your separation will mean to your children, it is important to bear in mind that children whose parents separate are liable to experience a complexity of relationships with adults in the remaining years of their childhood, and that these relationships will change over time. Their parents may get back together again, temporarily or permanently; many couples go through several attempted reconciliations before the marriage is ended or, more rarely, reinstated. Children may live with their mother but have more or less close contact with their father. They may live sequentially only with their mother, with their mother and a lover or series of lovers, with their mother and a permanent partner, or with their mother and a stepfather. Any of those men may, or may not, function as father figures for them, and any of the men may, or may not, bring children of their own to form a melded family with yours. At the same time, the absent father may become the one they live with, and whether this happens or not, they may move through a similar set of relationships that may or may not bring them an extra mother figure and/or children who are formally or informally their stepbrothers and -sisters. Eventually, there may be half-siblings, too.

MAKING THE BEST OF A BAD JOB

Nothing you can do will prevent parental separation from hurting your children, but thanks to research studies carried out in the past fifteen years, parents who separate today (and their advisers) can do better by children than those of even one generation ago; better, probably, than your own parents did by you if they are separated. You can do better, and if you can, you surely should. There is new and ongoing research into children's development, especially their emotional and social development, that can help you to understand what your separation means to

NEW FAMILIES IN OLD MOLDS

"Modern Western families no longer fit the conventional nuclear family mold. . . . Once-nuclear families may re-form, once or several times, involving and excluding not only various parent figures and perhaps half- or step-siblings, but also their relations. If a man comes to live with a divorced woman who has two children, does his mother become their grandmother? Can he, himself, be their stepfather if there is no marriage? If so, how long must he be in residence before he graduates into that role from being the mother's lover? And if there is a marriage, does he, the stepfather, remain part of the children's family if their mother divorces him?"

Source: Leach 1994

each one of your children and offers easily understood scientific information about ways of handling it that are likely to modify or curtail ill effects.

We know how lastingly important family breakdown and parental separation is for children, and we know some ways in which its impact can be minimized, right from the start. We know a great deal about what children and young people of different ages can be expected to understand about the separation and something about how to make it clear, day after week after month, that the separation is in no way the child's fault or a reflection of lack of love. Above all, we have real evidence to guide those difficult decisions about where and with whom children should live and how an absent parent can still be a mother or father. This kind of information, collected and delivered with children's perspective always in the foreground, is badly needed because without it children may—and often do—suffer unnecessarily. When people say that it's "only fair" for a father and mother to have the children living with each of them for the same number of days in the year, they mean that it is fair to the parents, not that it is necessarily fair—or likely to be appropriate—for their children. And a lawyer who encourages a client to try to insist on having his baby or toddler spend every weekend with him may not even be aware that such overnight separations from the mother are very likely to be distressing to such a young child and may even be damaging to his attachment and the brain development that partly depends on it.

Information about children in separating families *in general* cannot be a prescription for your family in particular, of course, because every member of every family is unique, and what works for one won't work, or be possible, for another. But there are now at least a few research-based dos and don'ts that seem to apply to all children of a particular age and in a particular circumstance. It will always be worth your while to think about such guidelines because they will usually be a much better bet for your children than having the two of you thrashing aimlessly about in all-night arguments or taking contradictory chunks of advice from relatives and friends who have axes to grind and sides to take. However, this kind of research will only really help you to help your children if you make a point of thinking about each child individually and keeping them securely tucked away in a corner of your mind all the time, now and in the several years it will probably take before you all settle into new family structures. That is much easier said than done, especially while your own feelings and arrangements leave so little space for anything else, but it's the foundation of all the kinds of help that you can give them.

> **Girl, aged eleven**
>
> "My mom did write once a week, but lots of the other girls had letters and parcels and phone calls and visits all the time. . . . I told myself she was busy with her new life. I was glad for her. Yes, I truly was. I'd been so worried for her when she was so unhappy. But I felt I'd vanished."

An eleven-year-old girl, the middle child of three girls, was sent to boarding school because her furious father couldn't—and didn't pretend he wanted to—look after her, and he would not allow her to live with her mother and mother's lover (future stepfather). Her older sister escaped to drama school; her much younger sister was allowed to stay with Mom. This child felt herself to be out of sight and out of mind.

The easiest way to preserve that vital space in your head for everyone is to make a clear separation in your mind between woman–man and child–parent relationships (see chapter 4). That means you don't express (and try not even to show) the hurt, miserable, angry feelings that belong to your sexual relationship rather than your parenting. Your ex-husband may be a complete letdown as a husband; a hopeless provider; a faithless, insensitive man; a complete bastard. But what is he as father to your child? Not "ex," to begin with (the two of you may be getting divorced, but he's not divorcing the child), and given the chance, he's very likely not to be a letdown or faithless or insensitive either. One of the things that women who are separating often find most painful to accept is that their children still love and should love the man they call Daddy.

Working out how to share parenthood when you no longer share a household is often a personal and practical minefield—as we shall discover (see chapter 5). But whatever the issues between you, and however you resolve them now and in the future, do

---

A CLOSE RELATIONSHIP WITH THEIR FATHER MATTERS MORE FOR CHILDREN THAN WHAT HE DOES

A review of research studies between 1987 and 2007 showed that children in intact families who had close relationships with their fathers did better in almost every way than those who did not. One study, for example, followed 8,441 infants of both sexes to the age of thirty-three and showed that those with closely involved father figures had higher levels of education and more close friends of both sexes and were less likely to smoke or to have had trouble with the police. Another study showed that women who had had good relationships with their fathers at the age of sixteen grew up to have better relationships with their husbands and a greater sense of mental and physical well-being.

Source: Lewis and Lamb 2007

remember that you are both the parents of this child or these children and that you are mother and father, not mother and (male) junior mother. You are different people in different roles, and however well or badly you each fulfill your role, both of you are crucially important to your child.

Recent American, Australian, and British research has made a big contribution to our understanding of what parental separation means to children by studying families over a period of years, not only when they are in crisis. Thanks to this large and growing body of work, we are beginning to accumulate what most of the research community would accept as "facts." Not every point may be accurate or relevant for your children or the children with whom you are concerned, but taken overall these are the nearest we have to hard information.

- **Separation/divorce makes children miserable.** Children who are too young to understand what is going on between their parents often adamantly refuse to believe in the fact or permanency of a separation. Whatever you tell them, you will probably need to repeat it, again and again.

   Older children who do understand that a separation is planned or permanent usually bitterly resent it. It seems clear that however poor the relationship between their parents has been, almost all children would prefer it to continue. Many dream of and work for reconciliation. The only exceptions researchers have found are among the few children who are physically terrified of the departing parent. They, and only they, may be relieved to see him or her depart.

These findings do not mean, of course, that a marriage that is not working should be held together "for the children's sake" (children may be unwise in what they wish for), but the findings do mean that if you are separating, you cannot assume that your children—even those who are almost grown-up—will agree that the family would be better split up than constantly quarreling.

- **Children tend to take guilty responsibility upon themselves for parents' breakup.** Younger children in particular, unable to fathom much of the reality of an adult sexual/habitual/ cooperating relationship, tend to assume that they caused it to disintegrate. It is difficult for a child, whose whole life centers

> **Boy, aged eight, when asked,**
> **"So what was the thing that made**
> **Daddy so angry?"**
> **"Drinking my Coke in bed."**

around his relationship with you, to realize that the same is not true of you: that swathes of his parents' lives are entirely separate from him. Furthermore, much of the friction that he has seen has probably involved his own behavior—his noise or his discipline, his mother's spoiling or his father's neglect—so he easily sees these accumulated small issues as the cause of the crash.

There may be subtler reasons for guilt, too. Young children are sexually aware. In the normal course of early development, they dream of partnership with the person of the opposite sex whom they love most (mother for a boy; father for a girl) and therefore fantasize about ousting the present partner (the other parent). The little boy who has secretly dreamed of "looking after Mommy" if only Daddy didn't get in the way sees Daddy's departure not only as a practical disaster but as evidence of his own wicked and terrifying power: he wished him away and now he wishes he had not. The little girl whose father leaves is similarly placed: clearly her love object has left because it was wicked of her to want to take her mother's place. The young child who is beset by this kind of guilt will be liable to separation anxiety, too (see chapter 8). Since her wickedness has caused one parent to leave the home, isn't it horribly likely that the other parent will also leave? At its mildest, such anxiety tends to make children cling to home and keep a too-careful eye on their mothers' movements. At the other extreme, it may make them feel so totally wicked and unlovable that they become convinced that neither parent can love them and that total abandonment is inevitable.

Older children, who have lived through the normal developmental stage of longing to replace the same-sex parent and have begun, instead, to identify themselves with him or her, are liable to a different sort of guilt. The separation makes them angry: angry, very often, with that same-sex parent. Whatever explanations they are given for the ending of the marriage, they tend to feel (as do others outside the relationship) that the parent could have done better. A boy may feel that if he'd been his father he could have remembered to phone when he was working late or could have spared one weekend day for the family; a girl may feel that if she'd been in her mother's place she could have held her tongue and avoided nagging. However justifiable that anger may be, it leads in its turn to more guilt and to anxiety: guilt over lack of sympathy with the same-sex parent, and anxiety because if those real feelings were known, surely the parent who has stayed with the family would leave, too.

> **Boy, aged twelve**
> "I couldn't bear him having to skulk on the street corner when he met us, but if he came to the house, she looked all pained and long-suffering."

> **Girl, aged fifteen**
> "I wanted to call him, tell him things that had happened, you know? She never stopped me, never said anything, but if she came in and I was on the phone to him she'd sort of go out, looking funny."

> **Boy, aged fourteen**
> "She'd ask me to do things, jobs around the place, and sigh because he hadn't done them before. I hated that; hated her for trying to make me feel I was better than him."

> **Girl, aged thirteen**
> "You'd have thought she was the only one it mattered to. I just kept feeling: 'OK, I can see you're really bummed, but what about me?'"

■ **Children tend to feel shut out by separating parents.** Most children, of all ages, crave attention from parents—often more attention than they easily get. The more involved parents are in couple business the less attention they may be able to spare for parent business. When separation actually takes place, many parents (understandably) become so involved in their own feelings that they cannot remain engaged in their children's everyday lives and cannot acknowledge the reality of their children's mourning for the loss of the absent parent.

To make matters worse, the parent who stays with the family is often as *emotionally* absent as the other parent is physically apart. Left with neither parent wholly present, children feel unsupported and yet are aware that their own concerns about everyday life and care are trivial as compared with all this high adult emotion.

> **Boy, aged sixteen**
> "Sometimes I'd say, 'Dad would have let me do such and such,' and she'd say, very politely, 'If your father had wanted to be the one to say what you should do, I think he'd have stayed around.'"

■ **Split loyalty is agony.** Children who suffer from it most are those whose parents make it acute by encouraging them to take sides. A few parents actually try to enlist children against their ex. Many more imply, often rather subtly, that any communication a child has with an absent parent is disloyal (see chapter 6).

While some conflict of loyalties is probably inevitable, a few of the points made by adolescents during interviews highlight the pain it can cause (see facing page and above).

■ **Many children *worry* about the absent parent.** For young children in particular, exclusion from the warmth and safety of home and family seems a horrendous exile and the fact that Dad left voluntarily is either beyond their comprehension or makes no difference to the fact that they worry about how he will manage alone.

Three- to ten-year-olds in particular ask:

Where will Daddy sleep?
Who will cook his dinner?
Who is looking after Daddy?
Isn't he lonely? Doesn't he miss us?
Has he got a television? Will he watch *The Simpsons*?

Mothers who share this kind of concern for the departed partner (or can find in themselves the generosity to acknowledge the reality of the child's concern) and can offer practical reassurance that "Daddy's OK" do children an important service. As soon as it is possible, children should see for themselves that the father's living circumstances *are* "OK."

■ **Children need parents to talk and to listen.** Research suggests that as many as one in five parents who are planning to separate are so flummoxed by the question "What shall we tell the children?" that they don't tell them much more than "He's gone and good riddance." Children whose parents discuss with them what is happening in the family and ask how it makes them feel not only survive the immediate shock better but also adapt more easily to the new circumstances.

Do your children know what's going on? Well, yes and no. They probably know something's happening because Daddy's not living with the rest of you; they can see when you've been crying; they realize Granny is furious though they are not sure who with, and when the dinner burgers get burned and there's no cereal left for breakfast three days running, it's obvious that their meals aren't claiming your attention. What they cannot know unless you tell them is what it is that is happening and why. Tell them. Trying to pretend that everything is the same as usual when it clearly is not will only increase their uneasiness and sense of insecurity; and the fact that your separation is long-term is not something you can conceal from them for long. Once you have managed to tell them that Mom and Dad aren't going to live together in the same house anymore, find age-appropriate words to tell each child why. Telling them nothing is not an option, because if you don't tell them at least a version of the real reason, they will invent reasons for themselves, and their fantasies will probably be worse than the reality.

The truth—perhaps that he, or you, have fallen in love with somebody else, or that he is more taken up with gambling than earning money for the family, or that you just don't love each other anymore—may seem brutal, but half-truths or lies will eventually be exposed, and

Girl, aged thirteen
"She was unhappy—OK, I know that—but she was always sighing: over money or how hard she was working and all that. Every sigh and everything she said was sort of a dig at him."

Girl, now aged eleven, looking back to when she was five
"She just said Daddy didn't want to live with us anymore. She didn't say why, but I knew it was because he didn't like me because I wasn't a boy and I still wet my bed."

then the children will have to face your untrustworthiness as well as the reality of what actually happened.

And there's another truth that you must give your children, no matter how difficult you find it to say: both of you still love them. Whatever the circumstances, whatever hurt you adults have caused each other, that is between the two of you and does not involve your children.

WHAT YOU BOTH SAY TO your children is important, but what they say to you is equally so. Hearing and dealing with the pain your separation is bringing to your children can be so difficult that there is a temptation to brush aside their feelings about it, offering comforting words instead of keeping quiet and listening. Don't let yourself be tempted. Allowing, indeed helping, your children to express their anger and bewilderment, their fears and anxieties, will help them adjust to the new situation. And the more they can deal with their painful feelings in the here and now, the less likely those feelings are to bob up again and make emotional difficulties for them when they are older.

These conversations are not easy, and there is no need to pretend that they are. Children can accept adult grief and anger, and once they (older ones at least) know what is happening, they will expect you to be upset. If you can possibly manage it, though, don't make them feel that talking about the situation upsets you so much that they should never mention it again, and try to make it clear to them that however hurt you may be, you are not destroyed by what is happening. Somewhere inside you is a solid core of strength on which they can rely, now and always.

2

Children's Ages and Stages

C hildren's ages have a powerful effect on how they perceive and are affected by their parents' separation and therefore on what they need from you both. If you have more than one child, each of them has reached a different age and stage of development from the others. Even if you have only the one, she is at a different stage today than three months ago and will be different again in three months' time. So while your family is imploding, it's as important for you to try not to think or talk about your children collectively as "the kids" as it is for parents of twins to make a point of thinking and talking about the two children as separate people rather than as "the twins." These group references imply that everything that is going on is the same for all of them, which of course it is not. What is happening in your family will affect every child differently, so what you can best do to protect and support each one will be different, too. Concentrating on each child as a separate person will help you to make sure that you understand, and meet, their different needs.

Wishful thinking may make you inclined to underestimate the impact of your separation and the horrible strains that probably preceded it on your child or children, whatever their ages. However, research suggests that you are most likely to under-

DO PARENTS ALWAYS KNOW WHAT CHILDREN FEEL?

Recent research suggests that just as parents are inclined to overestimate their children's intelligence or how much they exercise, so they tend to underestimate their children's unhappiness or anxiety—whether about parental separation or anything else. Special research materials were designed so that instead of relying on parents' reports of their children's feelings, children—between the ages of five and ten—could be asked directly about their emotional lives. The children's answers gave a much less rosy picture of their happiness and well-being than the answers given by their parents.

Source: Lagattuta, Sayfan, and Bamford 2012

estimate the distress of the two age groups at the extremes of childhood: babies and toddlers at one end and teenagers and young adults at the other. It's much less likely that you will miss signs of unhappiness, bewilderment, and anger in the age groups in between—elementary school and middle school aged children—because while they are often reluctant to talk about *what* is the matter, they usually make it all too clear that something is bothering them with noisy protests and "difficult" behavior at school as well as at home. Babies are different. As long as your baby is being adequately taken care of by familiar people in ways she is used to, she may seem unaffected by adult upheavals, or if there are signs of distress—such as lots of new night waking—they can easily be attributed to that first molar coming through. Teenagers are different again, especially those who are coming out of high school or are already at college. These almost-adult children who

Mother of three children, aged three, seven, and ten
"The three-year-old has dropped all his most recent 'grown-up' stuff like using the potty. He's gone back to diapers and baby talk. The seven-year-old doesn't seem to care about her dad being gone; she's only worried about places and things: like will we have to move and will we take the cats. As for the ten-year-old, she's ignoring both of us, really, and clinging to school and friends; she seems to be trying to be a teenager."

scarcely spend any time at home even if they are still technically living there may seem too taken up with their own relationships to be much concerned with their parents'. Both of those assumptions are illusory, though, and helping the youngest and oldest children through family breakdown depends on you being aware of that.

Father of two children, aged eighteen and twenty
"Our older kid is at college and the younger one is taking a gap year, so I thought I'd waited long enough; they're too busy with their own lives to worry about ours. My ex says I'm dead wrong, though. She says home still really matters to them, and they're both really upset."

BABIES

In human development, what happens in the future always depends on what has happened in the past. Your baby is at the beginning of her life and what happens to her now will lay the foundations for the whole of it. She isn't going to remain a baby for long, either. If she's a few months old when you decide that your marriage or partnership is at an end, the chances are that she'll be a preschool child by the time things even begin to settle down, and how secure she is in herself and easy for you to relate to then will largely

Grandmother of a baby, aged nine months
"His dad keeps saying the baby can't understand a word of what is going on, but I still wish they wouldn't count on him not knowing anything's happening. Words aren't everything, and I can see him watching them both when they're arguing and noticing when his mom's feeding him his dinner but really thinking about something else."

depend on what has happened to her in between. So even if it's your four-year-old who is wetting himself and resisting going to pre-K, or your six-year-old who suddenly refuses to listen to a word you say and shouts back if you raise your voice, that apparently oblivious six-month-old needs at least as much of your thought and attention. If you both choose to accept that and act accordingly, fine. If you need some convincing, here's a quick outline of the neuroscientific research findings that demonstrate its importance, based principally on the work of Allan Schore.

Why the First Year Is Crucial

Brain Development

Your baby, like all human babies, was born with an unfinished, still largely primitive brain. At birth he had only one-quarter of the part of the brain whose eventual great size and complexity is what makes him human (the cerebral cortex). Three-quarters must grow and develop from birth through toddlerhood: amazingly rapidly in the first year, still fast in the second year, and only a little more slowly in the third. Wherever he is in his first year, your baby's brain is an unfinished project, and, like it or not, completing it is *your* project. He cannot do it for himself; it's up to you. His brain is going to grow, but how it grows and develops and functions doesn't only depend on the genes you passed on or the physical circumstances and care you give him; it also depends on your feelings and behavior toward him and the relationship that develops between him and each of his parents.

People have always known that babies' behavior is affected by the way they are treated, of course. After all, that's the basis of all parents' attempts to encourage some behaviors and discourage others (smiling and hugging the baby when he is pleased and smiley; frowning and moving him away when he grabs a handful of hair). But it's only in the last two decades that it's become clear that parents' behavior toward a baby affects something far more basic and lasting than his immediate behavior: it affects the actual structure and functioning of that rapidly growing brain and therefore the kind of person he will become and the way he will behave throughout his life.

Although the idea that how and whether you cuddle and comfort, play and talk with your baby permanently affects his brain is new and surprising, it makes very good sense once you've thought about it. Worldwide, babies flourish in a vast range of environments: from tropical forest villages to packed northern cities, from poverty and starvation to wealth and obesity and from secure adult affection to impatient rejection. Different environments and circumstances require different behaviors, but babies can't be born with brains that are ready to adapt to any particular one of myriad possibilities. If they were, their skulls would have to be enormous, far too big for natural birth or for newborn neck muscles. So, instead of brains so large that they have the potential for anything, babies are born with brains that are unfinished and adaptable to anything, which then grow with astonishing speed to make the best of the environment and circumstances in which they find themselves.

In the first days and weeks of life a baby's environment consists almost entirely of his mother, and his circumstances are hers. In fact, each baby in a newborn nursery is already somewhat fitted to the mother who carried and birthed him, and he will immediately begin to adapt to her handling and their environment and go on doing so whether parents want him to or not. A new baby cannot wait in limbo while his mother recovers from the birth or his father arranges to start paternity leave. That's why premature or sick babies in neonatal units need to have parents close by as well as those vital specialized nurses. From the time of his birth, a baby needs at least one adult who is devoted to him. If he has no such person, receives minimal or inappropriate adult attention, or arrives in a home that is a place of anger, strife, or even violence, his brain structure and chemistry will immediately begin to adapt defensively. He may develop extra strong fear and anger reactions or intense attack and defense impulses in the deep, primitive part of his brain that is already developed. If, as the weeks pass, his brain continues to be suffused with stress hormones, he may start to become hypervigilant, permanently prepared for "fight or flight" and disproportionately upset by small things.

On the other hand, if a baby is born to a mother who celebrates her, cuddles and plays with her, listens to her, laughs with her, and comforts her when she is upset, the connections that form in her brain will be very different. Because she can rely on an adult being available and aware of her feelings and ready to soothe and correct extremes of stress, fear, and anger, she'll be on the way to becoming someone who can cope with emotional extremes for herself and form close relationships with other people.

Attachment

Everyone knows that babies need adult care every minute of every hour of every day and week, and it is obvious that a mother (or someone who stands in for the mother) with a close and loving relationship with her baby has the best chance of meeting the demands of constant care without becoming bored or burning out. But while there is nothing new or remarkable about that, there is surprising new evidence of how far beyond the provision of physical necessities and into the emotional world that such care needs to go. When babies are born, the left-hand "thinking part" of their brains scarcely exists. The right side of their brains (and their newly separated bodies) experiences and reacts to deep primitive feelings: fear, anger, excitement, and misery. But they do not have the brain capacity to "regulate" those fierce feelings and tone them down or bring themselves back from terror or excitement to calm. Unless somebody who is committed and sufficiently devoted constantly checks on the baby's emotional state, keeping him in mind even when he is not in sight, and lends him her own emotional resources, he may be overwhelmed. There are few more horrible sounds than the increasingly hysterical crying of a young baby who is being ignored and left at the mercy of his own unmanageable feelings.

Attachment between a mother (it usually is the biological mother, but it can of course be the father or someone else who stands in for her and may be referred to as the "primary caregiver") and her baby is a two-way street. The mother finds herself tuned in to her baby's feelings, and those feelings—fear, for example—produce a reassuring response in her, which in turn produces a response in the baby, which she again picks up and reacts to. The two of them are a dyad: dancers, interdependent. The mother is attuned to the infant, keeping him always in her mind no matter what else she is doing, and responding to him with her own right-brain responses rather than with conscious thought. Her attunement is helped by his instinctive behaviors and characteristics, such as clinging and sucking and eventually smiling. It is out of that attuned relationship that secure attachment grows.

Attachment is a survival mechanism. All human beings have a built-in genetic predisposition to seek refuge with whomever they are attached to when they are alarmed. People continue to develop attachments throughout their lives: to other family members, especially fathers; to adults from outside the family such as teachers; to childhood and adolescent best friends; and eventually to adult sexual partners. But the first attachment, forged in the earliest months of life to the mother or other primary caregiver, is the crucial foundation for all that follow. A baby or toddler who is securely attached can explore and experiment freely, provided the person who is his "secure base" is available or trusted to become available if he needs her. Her readiness to give any help he needs increases his sense of security, and the assistance she gives models for him solutions to his current and future problems.

A very large, rapidly growing body of international research, which is not yet widely understood, shows that babies' secure attachment to their mothers or whoever mothers them, and the attunement and responsiveness of mothers to their babies, is crucial to all aspects of lifelong development: to emotional stability and mental health and to physical health as well. Furthermore, stress, including the stresses that lead to and result from insecure or broken attachments, may damage a baby's capacity to learn and may, in extreme instances, damage it forever. When researchers compare children of any age on any aspect of development—learning language, resilience when things go wrong, sociable play with other children—the tuned-in-ness and readiness to respond of their primary caregivers in the first year explains more of the difference between the children's achievements than anything else. It is a fact, not merely an opinion, that the more a baby experiences his mother or her substitute as attentive, responsive, and loving, the more he will flourish today and the more resources he will have to cope with difficulties tomorrow.

Mothers, Fathers, and Babies

Every human baby needs at least one special person to attach herself to. One is an absolute necessity and two are even better. All over the world the first special person (the "primary caregiver" in research-speak) is more often the mother than the father. Pregnancy and birth set women up for the role, of course, but so do some differences in the way female and male brains function. Research suggests that taking the human species as a whole, females are better than males at understanding and responding to the communications of babies who cannot yet speak. Of course that does not mean that every woman is better at this than every man. Whatever the genders of a particular couple, one of them will probably take more easily to this role than the other. Within some male–female couples, this may be the father rather than the mother, and, if circumstances allow, parents may organize their respective roles accordingly. Usually, though, the mother has the largest role and impact on the baby in the first year, with the influence of the father—provided he spends enough time with the baby to exercise it—strengthening dramatically in the second year. This makes sense to attachment researchers, who suggest that what babies need most in the first year is maternal reassurance and soothing, while in the second year exploration and understanding of the physical world comes to the fore and is supported by fathers' more exciting, more challenging play.

If both of you shared your baby's care from the beginning, her emotional life will be both richer and safer for not being vested in one person alone, but that doesn't mean that you will be interchangeable, so that if you split up the two of you can stand in for each other in your baby's life. However closely fathers are enmeshed in their lives, babies usually start out most relaxed of all with their birth mothers, perhaps due to long familiarity with their smells, heartbeats, and voices, as well as to the bliss of sucking. More and more scientific research is showing how important the relationship between mother and baby is during the first months. For instance, there are findings showing that it's the mother's loving responses to her during that period that raises the levels of the feel-good hormone serotonin in a baby's rapidly developing brain. If the two of them are separated, or if a mother is too depressed or sad or angry to feel loving and to offer those responses, the baby's serotonin levels and her happiness may remain low.

By four or five months of age, babies with the luxury of two available parents will often play favorites. Fathers, perhaps especially fathers who have *not* been continually involved in their baby's routine everyday care, may suddenly find themselves singled out for favor because their sandpapery faces, deep voices, and exciting play are new and interesting. But being flavor of the day doesn't make father into mother, or into a replacement for her.

FATHERS AND MOTHERS ARE DIFFERENT

Recent research shows that attachment to mothers and to fathers is qualitatively different. Secure attachment to mothers is promoted by the sensitivity of their care in the first year, whereas secure attachment to fathers is promoted by the quality of their play, and the way they support and gently challenge babies' and toddlers' explorations.

Source: Schore and McIntosh 2011

Secure attachment to mother or another primary caregiver is crucial to a baby's brain development and therefore to her whole future. Babies who don't have anyone who is really attuned to them, who perhaps receive efficient physical care but not much in the way of emotional response, or are looked after by a succession of caregivers, often do not develop as fast or as far as they otherwise might have done. And once a baby-mother attachment is under way, losing it, either partially or completely, always delays or distorts her development. If your marriage or your partnership is disintegrating while your baby is less than a year old, negative effects on her development are a real risk that you both need to be aware of.

However secure and reliable your relationship with your baby has been so far and however determined you both are to protect her from the upheavals in your marriage, parental separation puts the mother-baby relationship at risk. You used to have a uniquely close two-way interaction with your baby without even thinking about it. But that becomes a struggle if your failing adult relationship keeps distracting you (see chapter 5), and keeping your baby always in mind is a challenge when that mind is taken up with misery. There is even a risk that overwhelming adult problems and emotions may not only distract your attention from your baby but also put your attunement to her at risk. Being so much loved and needed may suddenly feel claustrophobic so that instead of taking her dependence for granted you may find yourself yearning for at least a little time when she needs nothing from you. You may even feel that it is your relationship with the baby

Mother of boy, aged eight months
"I'm trying really hard to keep everything the same for him. Like I take him to the playground every afternoon, but the minute I start pushing him in the baby swing, I start daydreaming. In fact yesterday I went on pushing him longer than he wanted and didn't realize he wanted me to stop until he was actually crying. I felt awful. But then a friend came later in the afternoon, and I put a DVD on so we could talk, just for a minute, only we went on talking so long that he dropped off to sleep and he hadn't even had his dinner."

that has cost you your relationship with her father, and he may agree.

It is all too easy to let yourself assume that as long as she is being adequately looked after physically, that's enough, and then to fall back on going through the motions of mothering, or perhaps adding extra hours at day care or even employing a caregiver. It isn't enough. You cannot build and maintain the security of your baby's attachment to you just by being her biological mother and arranging for her physical care. First love is about emotional rather than physical needs. Your baby doesn't just need a caregiver

Father of two children, aged eleven months and three years
"We were having dinner like we used to do, around the kitchen table, normal family stuff. I was helping James with his food, and my soon-to-be-ex and I were talking. It got a bit tense, and then suddenly James shut his mouth and turned his head away and wouldn't eat . . . It was as if he was angry. I think he was angry."

Mother of two girls, aged four years and six months
"Jemima's four and she's getting louder and louder. Everything she says is a shout or a yell, and the more I tell her to hush, the worse she gets. The only person she talks normally to is baby Jess. When I asked her why, she said, ''Cause you can't hear us; you only listen to the people on your phone.'"

to come and feed or change her when she's hungry or wet, she needs someone who bears her constantly in mind and comes when she is bored or lonely or uncomfortable; someone who notices when she smiles and smiles back, who hears when she "talks" and listens and replies; someone who plays with her and shows her things, bringing little bits of the world for her to explore. If you always do all those things anyway, you may be surprised to hear them described as important. You are so attuned to her that these are not things you think about but simply things that you do, "action without thought" in response to a baby whose thinking brain is not yet developed. If so, all well and good. These are the things that really matter to your baby. Sadly, though, they are the very things that are likely to be put at risk by an adult relationship tsunami.

FIRST ATTACHMENT: THE PRIMARY CAREGIVER

"To my mind there is one single 'primary' caregiver. A good definition of the primary caregiver is that, under stress, the baby moves towards this single person in order to seek the external regulation he/she needs at the moment. Under stress, the baby will usually turn to the primary caregiver, not the secondary caregivers. In most family settings, things are building with the father in the first year and he is definitely getting a good sense of who the baby is, but the primary bond in most cases is to the mother in the first year and then, in addition to her, to the father and others in the 2nd and 3rd years."

Source: Schore and McIntosh 2011

Baby Sharing

When a marriage or partnership breaks down there's a lot of dividing up and sharing to be done, but don't make the mistake of confusing the dividing of objects or money with dividing up people and relationships. You cannot make up to your baby for less attention from you by arranging for him to have more from his father or vice versa. "Shared Parenting" (see chapter 7) has nothing to do with your separation and is not a solution to the stresses of this time. You don't share the parenting of your children because you are parting but because you are both their parents: always have been and always will be.

Unless parents shared or reversed roles early in this first year, the mother is the primary parent, and, right now, hard though it may be for the father to acknowledge it, her relationship with the baby is even more important than his. Whatever is going on in their adult relationship, it is essential to the baby that both parents have a real understanding of the vital importance of a baby's relationship with her mother or primary caregiver and of the importance these months of primary care will have to the rest of her life. All the developments and milestones of this first year are waiting inside her. She has a built-in drive to master and practice

BABIES' ATTACHMENT HIERARCHY

"My read of the current research is that the child's first bond is to the primary caregiver's (the mother's) right brain. At a later point, the 2nd year, the child will bond to the father if he is also providing regular care. At this later point, separation from the father will also elicit a stress reaction from the baby, the same as it would with separation from the mother. The second attachment and separation reaction is thus occurring at a later point in time than it would for the mother. Expanding upon these ideas I've suggested that although the mother is essential to the infant's capacity for fear regulation in the first year, in the second the father becomes critically involved in both the male and female toddler's aggression regulation."

Source: Schore and McIntosh 2011

every aspect of being human, from making sounds, using her hands, and rolling over, to eating real food or sharing jokes. But the achievement of each aspect of her growing up is also in the hands of her mother or whoever stands in for her. The more that primary caregiver holds and plays and talks and sings with her, keeping her on track, balanced, interested, and busy, the more completely she will fulfill her potential for brain growth, development, and learning: her potential as a person. This is no time to be arguing about getting your fair share of time with your baby as if she were a meal that could be divided so as to feed you both. By all means agree to share your baby's parenting through and beyond your separation, but make sure you are both clear that what you will be sharing is not just her physical presence or care but your love and concern and responsibility for her.

Fathers, Mothers, and Toddlers

Facing the breakup of his family, one of the most difficult things a loving father needs to do is to acknowledge that right now being with her mother is more important to their baby than being with him. It's as important and as difficult as it is for an angry, perhaps betrayed and deserted, mother to acknowledge that the children still love their daddy. If you want your separation to hurt your baby as little as possible, though, you do need to accept the growing body of research clearly establishing that in the first year of life this is so. It takes true selflessness for a father to put his baby's feelings, and his soon-to-be-ex's ability to meet them, ahead of his own; but if you can accept the research evidence that you are likely to be second rather than first in line for your baby's initial attachment hierarchy, further research will reward you with evidence of the growing importance of father-child relationships as babies enter toddlerhood, as well as of the overall and lifelong benefits to children, adolescents, and adults of long-term relationships with fathers.

Three more sets of observations—and your own common sense—may further help to strengthen your resolve:

- The better that father and baby know each other in her first year, the closer the bond between them will be in the second year and later. If you want the closest possible relationship with your toddler, don't go off in a huff because right now she's still a baby and loves Mommy best.
- Forming a secure attachment relationship with your baby and maintaining it when she is a toddler doesn't depend on her spending whole days or overnights or weekends with you. It doesn't even depend on her spending time with you that is right outside her mother's orbit. The two of you can become securely attached just by spending enjoyable and predictable daytimes together. That, after all, is what the close attachments that often develop between grandparents and very small children are usually based on.
- If you are trying to make or strengthen your attachment relationship with your child, forcing her to leave her mother and go with you, whether it's for an afternoon or a weekend, is completely counterproductive for you as well as cruel to her. If

she cries and clings and eventually has to be handed over like a package or peeled off her mother and pressed into your arms, what she will remember is not the nice time she eventually had with you but the distress of that parting. Next time a visit comes up, she will be even more distressed, not because of anything you did or failed to do, certainly not because she does not, in her own infant terms, love you, but because she's reminded of her own painful feelings last time and anticipates feeling that way again.

Babies, Toddlers, and Shared Care

Since the late twentieth century, the enormous importance of fathers in children's lives has been increasingly recognized, and a growing—though still relatively small—number of men have become actively involved in hands-on care of their children within marriage and determined to make arrangements to share care after marriage breakdown (see chapter 7). Many of the professionals who work with separating couples believe that as long as both the mother and the father are willing and able to look after the children, arranging for each of them to share in the children's care serves both adult justice and child well-being. Indeed, there is a presumption in family law in English-speaking nations that care of children should be shared equally after family separation (see pp. 91–100). The underlying argument, vociferously supported by fathers' rights organizations, is that this is the only way to make sure that fathers remain an integral part of their children's lives after parents have separated. However, what "shared parenting" after separation or divorce should actually mean, in global family policy or in individual cases, is hotly debated not only by parents but by a range of professionals.

Equal shares of children's time and care are rare, though, even when parents are willing to cooperate with each other. Fewer than one in fifteen children are based with the father rather than the mother, and whatever the legal agreement, most children spend more time with their mothers than with their fathers. For children of school age, the geography and scheduling of their school lives usually have a major impact on shared care arrangements (see chapter 4). The practical potential for more or less equally shared care is greater for younger children—for babies, toddlers, and preschool children—than for older children, and this is unfortunate. Since the mid-1990s, a great deal of research regarding parental separation and these youngest children has been carried out, principally in Australia as well as in the United States. Findings are debated but strongly suggest that shared care that includes spending nights away from the principal caregiver and "home" may not be in children's best interests and needs to be planned with caution and especially with attention to the existing relationship between the child and the nonresident parent.

IMPACT OF SHARED CARE ON BABIES AND TODDLERS

- Babies and toddlers under two years of age who spent one or two nights a week with a nonresident parent were more irritable than children who were primarily in the care of one parent, and they were also more watchful and wary of separation from that primary caregiver.
- Children aged two to three who spent five or more nights every two weeks with a nonresident parent showed significantly lower levels of persistence with routine tasks, of learning, and of sociable play than children who were primarily or entirely in the care of one parent in one place.
- The extreme attachment distress of regularly separated toddlers could be seen in their relationships with the primary parent. Some became very upset, crying or clinging to the parent; others became aggressive, hitting, biting, or kicking. A few developed eating problems such as food refusal or gagging.
- No ill effects of being "time-shared" between parents were evident in children past their fourth birthdays.

Source: McIntosh 2012

Of course not every child under four who spends some nights away from her mother (or other primary caregiver) will show any ill effects; but some will, and unless that caregiver is actually incapable of caring for the child full-time so that the only alternative is extended family or foster care, it is doubtful whether any child under two will actually benefit from spending some nights with one parent and some with the other.

IF YOU ARE THINKING about or struggling with shared custody that includes overnights for your baby or toddler, these are warnings to be heeded. Asking yourselves and each other the questions below may help you to decide whether or not this particular child in your particular family is likely to be able to tolerate moving between two parents and flourish in two homes.

Who Is This Child?

How old is she? A three- or four-month-old baby may not be obviously distressed by separation from her mother into her father's care because her attachment to her mother is not yet fully formed and exclusive. However, while such a young baby may not be visibly upset, there is a serious risk that frequent separations will disrupt her primary attachment to her mother and its security. Taking childhood as a whole, older children sustain separations better than younger ones, but this is not the case in this youngest age group, where two- and three-year-olds appear to be especially vulnerable.

What sort of person is she? Is she easygoing or anxious? Sociable or shy? Easy or difficult to comfort once upset?

Is there an older sibling who will be transferring with her from one home to another? Overnights appear to be easier for young children when they have an older sibling going with them to ease the transition (see pp. 53–55). Be careful, though. While the bond with an older sister or brother may be an important support to the younger child, being expected to be supportive may be an added burden to the older sibling.

What sort of relationship does the child have with each parent? The more securely she is attached to at least one of you—say her mother—the better she will be able to cope with spending time with her father, provided that he can provide warm, responsive care. If the child is securely attached to both parents and readily turns to each of you for comfort, then she should be able to switch between you relatively easily. On the other hand, if the nonresident father and the child are not securely attached to each other, and she does not confidently turn to him for comfort or reassurance when her mother is not there, overnight stays will be inadvisable and extremely stressful.

What were the parenting arrangements for this child before the separation? If one parent has always been the primary attachment figure while time with the other parent has been sporadic or disrupted or even nonexistent, only limited, brief, daytime visits should be attempted until a secure relationship has formed.

A baby's or toddler's happiness and security in a divided family and two homes is not up to her, of course; it is up to you—and is by no means easy to achieve. Whatever she is like as a baby personality, and however ready she may seem to be to use a secure attachment to her mother as the basis for security with her father also, the success or failure of shared care in two homes depends on how each of you feels and behaves—separately and together.

What Kind of Parents Are You?

Does each of you have a secure and warm relationship with the child that pre-dates your separation? If your fathering was formerly hands-off, you cannot hope to transform yourself overnight into a secure attachment figure and competent practical parent; it will take time and practice. Equally, if your mothering was mostly confined to after-work "quality time" and otherwise supported by a live-in housekeeper or nanny who can no longer be afforded, you and the child both face unimaginable upheaval, separately and together.

Are both of you genuinely supportive of each other's relationship with the child? (See pp. 108–13.) If you want her to be equally happy and secure with each of you, you'll both take never-ending care to be positive and reassuring to her when she's transferring from one of you to the other.

As a nonresident father, are you confident that you can maintain your child's consistent and predictable routines while she is staying with you? That means knowing what and how and when she eats, plays, bathes, and sleeps, which cuddly animals or other comfort objects share her bed, and which songs or stories end her day. Even if you were a hands-on participant father who knew every detail of his child's life until you moved out of the family home a few months ago, those are not details you can take for granted now. Children grow and change, and at this stage in their lives they do so amazingly fast. Since you last put your daughter to bed, Pink Piggy might have made way for Dragon.

Is your relationship with your ex essentially conflict-free? If conflict should arise, you should both be determined to ensure that it does not take place within sight or hearing of the child.

Do both of you monitor and discuss your child's reactions to the repeated and recurrent separations? If either of you should run into problems, even in the middle of the night, you should feel able to telephone for the other parent's advice.

Unless you can both come very close to meeting these ideals, your child will be better off if you make arrangements for sharing her parenting that do not involve her in spending nights away from home, at least until she approaches pre-K age.

TODDLERS AND PRE-K CHILDREN (EIGHTEEN MONTHS TO FIVE YEARS)

Even if they are not expected to divide their time between two parents and homes, children between, say, eighteen months and five years usually react to parental separation with a mixture of grief and rage. And although the older children of any other age group tend to cope more robustly than the younger ones, that is not the case here. It is often children around the age of three who react most negatively.

Early toddlerhood is a stage of development when all children, even those in the most secure and predictable families, tend to suffer from "separation anxiety": the fear of being lost by, or of losing, a parent. At this age your child's brain is only just becoming able to hold on to an image of you when he can't see you, and therefore he is only just beginning to understand that when you go away you still exist and will come back. In the meantime he naturally wants to keep an eye on you and to go with you wherever you go. If you want two minutes of privacy in the bathroom, you have to pick your moment or put up with him thundering on the door.

When one parent—let's be realistic and say Daddy—moves out and is no longer there to do the parenting things he used to do, like read the bedtime story or help with dressing in the morning, he really is lost to the child. Lots of visits in the daytime over the next months, combined with his young brain's maturing, will gradually help the child to believe in his vanishing father's continued existence and to have confidence in his reappearances, but in the meantime he will probably experience daily life as a miserable muddle, especially as, having lost Daddy, he is desperately anxious about losing Mommy (see chapter 8).

Whether your toddler is a boy or a girl, he or she is likely to cry far more often and for longer than before the breakup and to be extra-demanding of adult attention. If the child is a boy, he may suddenly seem to become both angry and restless as well as sad. Don't be surprised if teachers at day care tell you that he withdraws from his former friends, spending a lot of time sitting alone, and that when he does join in group activities he is difficult and disruptive. Some girls react to their parents separating in a similarly sad and angry way, but other girls cope completely differently. You may find yours suddenly behaving like a very small adult, trying to take care of herself instead of seeking adult help, and perhaps becoming worryingly concerned with being "a good girl" and keeping her clothes clean.

Insecurity, anger, and sadness make a potent mixture, which, in a large enough dose, can slow up, halt, or even reverse the most recent and grown-up developments of this not-quite-baby-not-yet-child age group. Newly dry beds may be wet again, the potty rejected in favor of a diaper. Demands may be made for help with eating, for milk in a bottle rather than a mug, or for a pacifier, and whenever you go out, there may be endless requests to ride in the stroller or be carried rather than walk. Your child demands more of you just when it would be easier for you if you could give less. And if you do give less—because you can't help it—the demands will escalate.

Even under the most peaceful family circumstances, adults often find toddlers and pre-K children difficult to live with, and the circumstances of family breakdown are far from peaceful.

Do try your best to stay on your toddler's side. Although she can understand what "no" means and recognize when you are annoyed with her, she doesn't yet understand *why* you approve and disapprove of particular behaviors, which means that she is

---

LEARNING HOW TO BEHAVE

"Children are noisy, messy, untidy, forgetful, careless, time-consuming, demanding and ever-present. Unlike even the longest-staying visitor they don't ever go away. They can't be shelved for a few weeks when you are extra-busy, like a demanding hobby; can't even be ignored, like pets, while you sleep late on Sunday, because they have an unfailing ability to make you feel guilty. The guilt trips that come with children are worse than the upturned cereal bowls, bitten friends or walls drawn on with lipstick. Loving children (as almost every parent does) magnifies the pain of them as well as the pleasure. Loving them may even make it difficult for you to admit that they are sometimes a pain."

Source: Leach 2010b

nowhere near ready to cope with your anger or disappointment or sadness when she doesn't cooperate. If you are angry with her, she will certainly be upset, but she won't learn anything useful from it because the reasons for adult feelings and behavior are still a complete mystery to her, so your anger seems to her as meaningless but terrifying as a thunderbolt.

Between ages two and three, a growth spurt may mean that she suddenly looks more like a child than a toddler, but the saddest mistake you can make is to think of her, or to treat her, as more grown up than she actually is. Above all, don't let yourself expect her to understand that you are having a tough time and need her to be "good." If you and she keep quarreling, think through the last occasion—breakfast perhaps—from her point of view rather than from your own. She didn't know—couldn't know—that spilling her mug of milk so it splashed the sleeve of her sister's clean school shirt was "the last straw" for you on a really bad morning. She didn't know that it was a bad morning or what that means. If she sensed anything at all as you raced around the kitchen, late and multitasking, eyes still swollen from last night's tears, she will only have sensed your general tension, and although she will have disliked it, she will neither have understood what it was about nor even wondered. She doesn't understand much about your feelings or your life because she hasn't had enough experience yet, and the part of her brain that enables empathy is only now developing.

IT MAY BE HELPFUL to realize that the difficulty you are having in coping with a child in this age group when you are already highly stressed is not due to her bad behavior but to your general irritation with her childishness. It will help the child, because if she cannot be childish when she is two years old, or four, when can she be? It will help you not to decide that she is especially disobedient, ill-disciplined, and spoiled, and therefore you won't blame yourself for being a bad parent—which is the biggest guilt trip of all. And it will remind everyone who has any contact with your child—from grandparents and babysitters to preschool teachers—not to stick on her the problem labels that so easily become self-fulfilling prophecies. If your child believes that you or her father think she is naughty and nasty, she will live up to that view and probably come to share it herself and make sure that her teachers do, too. So try to hang on to the truth, which is that she is very young, that family life is especially difficult right now, that you aren't perfect and shouldn't expect yourself to be, and that things will change for the better. You can count on that because your child is going to grow older, easier to communicate with, and more able to understand.

KINDERGARTEN/ELEMENTARY SCHOOL AGED CHILDREN (FIVE TO SEVEN YEARS)

Many rising five- to seven-year-olds do seem to react to family breakdown differently from children who are a year or two younger or older. In both sexes the main reaction at this point is usually sadness, without the anger that younger children often display. Many teachers (and even classmates) report that these children are "always crying," and when they are asked what they are crying about, they usually answer straightforwardly, "I miss

---

SCHOOL-AGE ATTACHMENTS

Many children behave very differently with parents in their homes and with unrelated caregivers elsewhere, and the nature of their attachment relationships with the adults in each setting will usually be part of the explanation. By school age, though, most children have arrived at one dominant style of attachment that applies in all their relationships, so a shy child will be noticeably shy in all settings while a secure child will take his confidence with him wherever he goes.

Source: Leach 1994

Girl, aged seven
"That was my nearly asleep dream, about Dad coming up the path with his wheelie and Mommy giving him a big hug."

Girl, aged seven
"When the phone rings, I always think it'll be Daddy coming home."

Boy, aged seven
"There's a concert at school and I'm IN IT, so this time they'll both come and they'll sit next to each other and then we'll all come home together."

Boy, aged four
"My daddy does the long grass 'cause Mommy can't. He washes his hands, and last time he had a cup of tea. But then he wented again."

Boy, aged five
"It's 'cause I woke up too early . . ."

Boy, aged seven
"I talked too loud. He always said 'Sshh' and I didn't."

Girl, aged eight
"They didn't want to get me from school. I heard them yelling about having better things to do."

my dad" or "I want my mom to come home."

But the crying is unlikely to be only about missing a parent. These children are overwhelmingly sad because they assume that a parent who has moved out of the shared family home has rejected them. Many in this age group are mature enough to seek an explanation for the parental breakup, but only the exceptional child will look in the right place—the relationship between the parents. Almost all will assume that the whole horrid upheaval is their fault. Daddy has gone to live somewhere else because they are unlovable and unloved.

As well as blaming himself for the parent's absence and missing him or her, your child may also be deeply worried about both of you and will almost certainly be desperately hoping to get you back together again.

If your child is feeling like this, there is a real risk of depression and a high probability of a drop in performance at school and in any after-school activities. Boys in this age group whose fathers leave home are likely to be even more distressed than girls even if fathers regularly visit, and there may be complaints about their behavior at school, adding to their feeling that they are bad boys whom nobody loves.

ELEMENTARY SCHOOL AGED CHILDREN (EIGHT TO ELEVEN YEARS)

If sadness is the predominant emotion in most rising five- to seven-year-olds whose parents separate, anger often overwhelms it in this older age group. Your child may be intensely angry with one or both of you during and after the breakup of the family. He or she is likely to take sides against which- ever parent is seen as having fractured family life, often seeming to take pleasure in apportioning blame. Very of- ten, of course, a child's lim- ited understanding of the

> **Girl, aged ten**
> "When we're at school, she's all by herself. Nobody to help her with stuff, go to the store for her, or answer the phone. OK, my dad was at work but he was coming home. Now he isn't. She doesn't cook dinner like she did, and I don't know what she will do."

situation means that he or she blames the wrong parent. You may discover that your son blames you for forcing his father to leave the family home when the reason you took a stand was an ongoing affair. Unfortunately, their interest in which parent was at fault makes children in this age group especially vulnerable to parental blame and revenge games (see chapter 6).

However angry your child may be, though, anger will not be his or her only reaction to the family upheaval. Although people often describe children as self-centered, egocentric, and selfish, many children in this age group are also enormously concerned for their parents' well-being, frightened about what is going to happen to them, and lonely for the people they used to be. Even

Boy, aged nine
"He hasn't got a proper house or his garden or his shed. He's just got a little room and he's all alone in it with nothing to do and nobody to talk to. Mom says not to worry; he'll just be out at bars, but I don't think she means it nicely."

at this young age, many also try to take care of the parent with whom they are living, acting like parents themselves and trying to make things better for the adult.

More than anything else in the world, most children want the family breakdown not to have happened or, failing that, want their parents to get back together again. But no matter how passionately they want things to change, they are powerless to change them and, deep down, they know they are. Furthermore, this is an age when children's social lives and their desire to conform to the peer group are becoming increasingly important. Should they tell their friends about the parental separation? What will they think? And if they don't tell, how can they explain why Saturday's sleepover and their June birthday party are at different addresses?

Children want to be in control of who tells what to whom, but they are unlikely to be able to manage it for themselves.

CONFIDING IN PEERS

Findings from research based on data from longitudinal studies, such as the National Institute of Child Health and Human Development Study of Early Child Care and Youth Development and The Development of the Person: The Minnesota Study of Risk and Adaptation from Birth to Adulthood, consistently show that the security of children's early attachment relationships are predictive of their peer relationships later on. Children who have been securely attached since early infancy tend to have more and closer friends than insecurely attached children and are less likely to dislike or be disliked by others.

Source: Crittenden and Claussen 2000

If you are on friendly terms with the parents of your child's best friend or friendship group, offer to tell them what is going on so that they can tell their children. As for the school: the principal and school secretary need to know about the separation so that communications from the school are sent to each of you. But in addition, unless the child is strongly opposed to the idea, it will probably be helpful to talk to her class teacher, who is the adult best placed to keep a supportive eye on her and cut her a little slack when necessary.

> **Girl, aged eight**
> "I want Amelia to know I'm sad but I don't know what to say to her. 'My dad's gone' sounds really weird. It is weird, actually."

For children in this age group, there is about a fifty-fifty chance that his or her school performance will drop off along with self-confidence and ability to concentrate. As in younger age groups, boys are more susceptible than girls both to becoming withdrawn and to acting out their feelings with unacceptable behavior. Children of either sex may also react to the complex web of emotional distress that family breakdown causes with psychosomatic symptoms such as headaches and bellyaches. These are not made up; the pain is real, but its basic cause is emotional rather than physical. If psychosomatic complaints are a major feature of a child's reaction to the family breakdown, a visit to a (sympathetic) pediatrician may be helpful, because the child herself may be worried about her health and welcome reassurance that her symptoms are caused by sadness and stress rather than illness.

MIDDLE SCHOOL AGED CHILDREN (ELEVEN TO FOURTEEN YEARS)

Transferring from elementary to middle school is stressful for most children when home and family are stable, and for every child when the family is in crisis. Although your thirteen-year-old's concern about the situation may be less obvious than your nine-year-old's, it will probably be even more intense and potentially more hazardous.

Adolescence is a stressful period of development, and how your adolescent child reacts to the added stress of family breakdown depends not only on chronological age but also on the point he or she has reached in the development of puberty. Bear in mind that immature brain development means that teenagers tend to be emotional, impulsive, and liable to take risks without thinking through consequences.

Some adolescents who don't like what is going on at home partially disengage from their families and spend more time with their friends elsewhere. This can be a good adaptation or a risky one, and only you two can decide which is the case with your child. For a fourteen- or fifteen-year-old who has already

---

BRAIN DEVELOPMENT IN THE TEEN YEARS

There is overwhelming and still accumulating neuroscientific evidence that highly significant brain development takes place during adolescence, especially early adolescence—thirteen to fourteen years old. The key aspect of this is the marked immaturity of the neural networks of frontal brain regions implicated in planning, perspective taking, social understanding, and evaluating future consequences. The brain immaturity manifests in impulsive decision making, decreased ability to consider long-term consequences, engagement in risky behaviors, and increased susceptibility to negative influences.

Specifically, this body of research indicates that early adolescence marks the onset of puberty, heightening emotional arousability, sensation seeking, and reward orientation; that mid-adolescence is a period of increased vulnerability to risk taking and problems in affect and behavior; and that late adolescence is a period in which the frontal lobes continue to mature, facilitating regulatory and executive competence.

Source: Casey, Jones, and Hare 2008

achieved some personal autonomy and independence from his parents, effectively focusing on his own ambitions and plans and disregarding the parents' problems may be an adaptive way to react to family breakdown. But when a twelve- or thirteen-year-old who feels lonely without the accustomed family structure and is less carefully supervised than before (see pp. 198–211) takes refuge with groups of somewhat older peers, there is a real risk of him or her joining in with exciting risky activities often involving underage drinking, sexual activity, or drug taking, possibly coupled with shoplifting or other antisocial or illegal behavior.

An opposite reaction, seen almost exclusively among girls, pulls a teenager more closely into the family, coping with her own loneliness, confusion, and guilt by helping to run a fractured household or care for younger children.

IF YOU ARE STRUGGLING to work full-time as a single parent, your adolescent's willingness and competence may be crucial. But if she is expected to provide snacks and sympathy for younger schoolchildren and perhaps to complete the day's domestic chores and prepare an evening meal, make sure to acknowledge that in enabling you to do a full-time paid job she is doing a part-time one herself. She is in exactly the same position as she would be if she worked in a family business.

It can be very valuable to an older adolescent to feel that he or she is a necessary part of the home setup, but don't let yourself slip into dependence on that labor. There will come a time when he or she wants (and needs) either to leave home altogether or to transfer to "boarder" status while attending college or serving an apprenticeship. It is one thing for the adolescent to feel needed, quite another to know that his or her presence is literally indispensable. When he or she leaves school and finds a job, you must not ask, even silently and with your eyes, "Who will look after the little ones until I get home from work?" That must not be the adolescent's problem, because it is yours. You need to have foreseen both question and answer in advance. Leaving home is difficult enough for many youngsters without that kind of added stress.

In the meantime, however welcome her help and companionship may be, don't often let your daughter stay at home instead of going out with friends or help small siblings with their homework instead of doing her own. It is not her job to manage your problems; it is your job to protect her from them.

Many of the dilemmas and difficulties that are normal in families with teenage children are exacerbated by parental separation. Even in intact and stable families, for example, many adolescents of all ages and both sexes experience conflict between home life and peer group life. If most of every weekend is taken up with sports, the young person may see very little of his or her family; and if every Friday and Saturday night is for going out with friends, he or she will be left out of family birthday celebrations or special dinners. Balance and compromise are needed.

WHEN PARENTS SEPARATE, the need for that balance is doubled, but available compromises are often halved. Arrangements that ensure a child spends time with each parent—such as weekends with Dad—may work well when children are in elementary school but become intolerable to teenagers, who need to be allowed, even encouraged, to stick around and hang out with their friends. But at the same time that they are fighting against having to be away from home base every weekend, many adolescents will regret seeing less of the nonresident parent and feel guilty for not doing more to fill the empty partner-shaped space in each parent's life. Boys may feel that they ought to be "the man of the house," not only in the sense of changing lightbulbs or carrying heavy stuff but also in the sense of looking after the mother if she seems sad or lonely. Girls likewise often feel obligated to keep their fathers company. Sometimes such relationships become inappropriately romantic, even seductive, unless parents draw and maintain very clear lines between adult and child, parent and friend (see chapter 3).

HIGH SCHOOL STUDENTS AND YOUNG ADULTS (FOURTEEN TO EIGHTEEN YEARS AND ABOVE)

The depth of the effect parental separation or divorce can have on "grown-up" children is often overlooked or disbelieved. Older teenagers, perhaps those who are already away at college, spend few stretches of time at home and may seem only to make contact when they need something. Some parents accuse them of behaving like boarders or of treating the home like a hotel. Do be careful, though, that you do not *treat* your daughter or son like a boarder or a guest. The home—particularly their room or space within it—and family members are acutely important to them as the safe base from which they came and to which they can return when outside life gets too difficult. That safe retreat is the emotional and geographical place from which they can launch themselves into adulthood. The fact that your child doesn't spend much time in the home or with you does not mean that either has become unimportant.

Boy, aged eighteen

"My parents stayed together for me until I'd graduated from high school and started college. I didn't know that—no idea. When they told me they were splitting up and selling the house to buy an apartment each, they seemed to think I wouldn't care. No, worse than that: they seemed to think it was none of my business. I actually think that's why I made such a mess of everything."

Girl, aged eighteen

"Before I even left for college, Mom told me she was going to give my room to my sister so that she and my littlest sister had a room each and I could share with one of them when I came home. OK, it sounds kind of reasonable, I know, but I really minded so much, especially when she packed all my stuff up. My dad knew I was upset and eventually he asked if I'd like to make the room I stayed in at his house into my own. It was nice of him, but I couldn't really do that to my mom . . ."

It isn't uncommon for parents to struggle or drift on in a more or less loveless marriage "until the children leave home" and then split up. If you have stayed together "for the sake of the children," you might have given them stability, as you intended, but you might also have presented them with a very chilly model of adult relationships. And the breakup, when it comes, may not be any easier for these nearly adult children than it would have been years ago. If your teenager had thought—or assumed—that you were reasonably happy together (or hadn't given the matter any thought) and is now told that your separation has long been planned, he's liable to feel that if your relationship with each other was a lie, so was his whole childhood and his relationships with you. A later family breakup may have less impact than an earlier one in the here-and-now, but it has an enormous impact on the young person's sense of his own family history.

Try not to assume that at nineteen or even twenty your children are grown up enough to be able to "understand" why you have split up and to be "sensible" about it and "fair" to both of you. Above all, don't assume that because they have sexual relationships themselves they will sympathize with a parent's affair. Young people who are struggling to find themselves as adult men or

Young man, aged twenty-two

"First I really couldn't believe what they were telling me. Truly. I had a moment there when I thought it must be a joke. But then it sank in and it just sort of stole my childhood. OK, that sounds dramatic, but everything I'd known and trusted had been a lie, and they'd been waiting for me to get out of the way so they could smash it up. I stayed angry for years. Actually, I'm still angry. I'm not nearly as close to either of my parents as a lot of my friends are to theirs."

Woman, looking back

"When I was fourteen, my dad told me that one of the things he missed about my mother was her 'tip-tilted breasts.' Even as an adult and a parent myself I still cringe and can't forgive his crass insensitivity. Talk about 'too much information' . . ."

women are often very judgmental about the behavior of their parents' generation and usually intensely embarrassed if they are forced to acknowledge their parents' sexuality. You are their mother and father, not their friends. The less you confide in them, the better.

3

Other People, Inside and Outside the Family

S eparation and divorce aren't nearly such private matters as most couples think—or hope. Because our society and the care of the next generation are organized around marriage and monogamy, the breakup of a family touches many people directly. There may be close relations and relations by marriage who are deeply saddened for you both. Your own mother may wonder if she is partly responsible because she herself is divorced and brought you up without a father figure. In your own generation, there may be brothers or sisters who are alarmed for themselves, feeling that if your apparently solid marriage has foundered, their own may be at risk. A little further away there may be cousins and perhaps their girlfriends or boyfriends (and *their* families) who feel personally interested in what has happened and why. And then of course the breakup will be titillatingly interesting to almost every acquaintance who hears of it—and many will.

Not all these people will matter to your children, of course, but some will. Although parents are almost always the most important people in young children's lives and the most important adults all through adolescence, they are not the only ones.

When parents separate, having other people they are close to around—relatives or long-standing family friends—can make a tremendous difference both directly to the children themselves and indirectly because supported parents are more able to be supportive to their children.

SIBLINGS

The most important people to a child, outside the bust-up trio of himself, his father, and his mother, are usually siblings. During a parental breakup, it is bad luck to be an only child because children come through better if they have one or more brothers and sisters to share it with, whatever their ages and the age differences between them and even if they haven't been especially close up to now. In middle childhood and in adolescence, children may find it easier to talk to each other rather than to anyone else about what is going on. Where the age gap is too great for comfortable confidences, a younger sibling can simply feel cared for and an older sibling can feel caring. That often gives both children some of what they feel the breakdown of the family is taking from them: loving care.

Don't let yourselves rely too much on the relationships between your children, though. You are the grownups. It is all too easy to let the care an older child gives to a younger one become burdensome for her, and the fact that two teenagers support and confide in each other doesn't mean that they don't need to talk to both of you.

Girl, aged fourteen
"When our parents finally split up, I was eleven and Jack was eight and he really didn't like going to Dad's place on his own, so we always went together. But now he's eleven, he still always wants me to go, too, and often I really need to be around with my friends. Dad understands that. He'd be cool with me meeting him for lunch sometimes instead of spending all day, but Jack really needs me."

WHATEVER THEIR AGES and however close they may feel, your children are not responsible for one another; you and their father are responsible for them, and you may need to spell that out many times in addition to acting accordingly.

Above all, although you can count on simple companionship meaning that two or more children help one another to cope with this stressful time, don't assume, or let anyone, including the children themselves, assume that they feel exactly the same about the situation or aspects of it. One child may blame you for everything that's gone wrong while another blames her father. One may think his own bad behavior was responsible for his dad leaving, and another, enshrined as the family good kid, may thankfully agree because holding her brother responsible lets her off the hook. Later on, one child may love going to her father's house while another may find leaving you to spend time with him intolerable. Eventually, one may like the new stepmother while another blames her for the breakup or resents her attempts at mothering.

Boy, aged eleven
"She used to give me wine because she said she couldn't drink by herself. One day I told that to my dad and he was really, really pissed."

Boy, aged thirteen
"I know she's unhappy, but I wish she wouldn't tell me why. I think it's what's called 'too much information.'"

Girl, aged twelve
"Of course I knew he was lonely—he was so excited to see me on weekends that I couldn't ever say I wanted to stay at home for someone's birthday party."

You can't conjure up a sibling for your child, of course, any more than you can magically produce an extended family or support network. If there's only one child involved in your breakup, the particular things you need to watch out for depend very much on her age (see chapter 2). If she isn't yet pre-K age, she shouldn't be expected to be away from you overnight, though if she had a trusted older sibling, he or she might help to keep separation anxiety in check. If she is a teenager or college student, her companion and confidante would probably be a friend even if there was a sibling available. It's during the in-between years—say five to fourteen—that being the only child of a broken family may be especially difficult. Whichever parent the child is with, there are only the two of them, and it is easy for them to come to depend on each other for company and support. There are girls not yet in their teens who feel that they ought to look after their lone fathers, domestically and even romantically, and boys who try to be the man of the house for their lone mothers. Sometimes well-meaning but misguided relatives and family friends actually exhort children to look after their parents. Unfortunately, a single father or mother is often also lonely and all too willing to step out of the parent role to make a companion, even confidante, of the child (see chapter 5).

Father of girl, aged fourteen

"I had come to rely a lot on my friend Maria. She quite often came over and cooked a meal for us both at my place. She was dying to meet my daughter, so she came on Saturday meaning to do a nice dinner for the three of us, but Rhianna would hardly speak to her. When she saw Maria in the kitchen cooking, she went mental and said I obviously didn't need her so she was going home. I asked my ex if it had been tactless of me to have Maria there, and you wouldn't want to print what she told me!"

The more adult friends and supporters the parent has, the more likely it is that he or she will be able to see adult life as continuing even without the partner, and the easier it will be for the child to see the parent as OK and, hopefully, to relax and gradually relinquish the quasi-adult role. However, children in this situation can easily become jealous of anyone else their parent relies on, especially if it's a boyfriend or girlfriend.

GRANDPARENTS

Grandparents are very special to a lot of children, and children are very special to a lot of grandparents. Many grandparents are special to their grandchildren's parents (their own adult children), too. In fact the popular assumption that grandchildren are even more beloved than children does not bear examination. Much of what grandparents do for their grandchildren they do to please their children and be involved in their lives.

The importance of grandparents to families in the Western world, especially to children, is seriously underestimated. Grand-

---

GRANDPARENTS' CONTRIBUTION TO CHILDREN'S CARE

Throughout the English-speaking world and starting from babyhood, more children who need care while parents are at work get it from grandparents than from anyone else.

Once they had any regular care from anyone but the mother, around a quarter of the American babies in the National Institute of Child Health and Human Development study and a similar proportion of the English babies in the Families, Children & Childcare study were cared for by grandparents for an average of around thirty hours a week.

"By the end of babies' first year, neither father care nor grandparent care is quite so predominant because other types of care are used more frequently. Grandparents continue to provide a large proportion of the total, however—often a larger proportion than is immediately obvious from statistical tables. When children are in more than one type of nonmaternal child care, the second or 'extra' type is usually grandparent care. . . . When children were in what was termed 'combination care'—family day care, say, plus something else—the something else was almost invariably care by a grandparent. And when grandparents' contribution to 'combined care' was added to the category of 'grandparent care,' it became clear that grandparents were providing more child care than any other category of caregiver."

Source: Leach 2010a

---

parents who live close by often provide the child care that makes it possible for their daughter or daughter-in-law to work outside the home. Grandparents who live too far away to provide hands-on help quite often help financially instead. A few help with the down payment on a home. Some pay toward day care costs or help out with extras such as school trips or music lessons for an older child.

Even when grandparents are not their grandchildren's principal or secondary caregivers, and even if they undertake no regular child care at all, many still make a large—if largely unrecorded and therefore hard to quantify—contribution to those children's care and well-being, including making an incalculable contribution to the parents' ability to hold down a job. Even if they do not undertake regular child care, grandparents who live within easy reach of the grandchildren's home often serve as backup caregivers who can be called upon to step in when regular arrangements go wrong. Even grandparents who live hours of traveling time away are sometimes called upon to come and stay with children who are too ill to attend their regular child care so that parents need not take time off from work.

By no means do all grandparents welcome these commitments. They want to see and spend time with their children and grandchildren but would rather do so socially and when it suits them. Many speak sadly of having had to abandon retirement plans for leisure and travel. In a recent Australian study, some grandparents expressed open resentment at any assumption that they would take on the role of child care

Maternal grandmother of three children

"If I could say no without turning my daughter's work life upside down, and without losing my chance to see the kids and her regularly, I would."

provider for their grandchildren and objected to this role being expected of them by their children or the community.

However, a grandparent who stands in for or backs up parents in caring for a child while the family is intact, especially if they have done so from babyhood, is likely to be highly placed

GRANDFATHERS CARING FOR GRANDCHILDREN

When grandfathers reported looking after grandchildren, only 4 percent of those interviewed said they took the main responsibility of care, while around half shared it with their partner or spouse and nearly half said their partner or spouse was solely responsible for the grandchildren. In contrast, more than half (54 percent) of the grandmothers reported taking the main responsibility of care for grandchildren, with just over one-third saying they shared the responsibility with their partner or spouse.

Source: Millward 1998

in that child's attachment hierarchy. Mother will probably come first and Father next, but the third most important person in his life may well be a grandmother (or perhaps a grandfather), who will therefore be in an ideal position to help when the family breaks up.

In this generation many grandfathers have moved into new roles with grandchildren just as their sons and sons-in-law have become increasingly participant in their children's lives. Many are, and are expected to be, interested in their grandchildren as well as loving them, and their presence in the lives of father-deprived children can be invaluable. One grandfather, newly retired, expressed the sentiments of many when he said, "When my children were growing up, I was so busy making a living I had very little time for them. Now my biggest joy is being with my grandchildren. Maybe I'm trying to make up for what I didn't do before." However, although grandfathers, especially maternal grandfathers who have retired from work, often spend a lot of time with their grandchildren, even taking part in grandparent child care, they almost always do it in partnership with their wives. Very few grandfathers take sole or even main responsibility for the care of a grandchild, whether he or she is being looked after at home or taken out for a treat.

GRANDPARENTS ARE IMPORTANT not only to babies and toddlers. A large survey, published in 2012, of grandparents providing care to grandchildren in the United States showed that more than 60 percent provided grandchild care over the ten years of the study (1998–2008); 70 percent of those continued for two years or more. Grandparents with more economic resources and fewer health issues were the most likely to offer care.

And grandparent care does not necessarily end even when children reach school age. In Australia in 2002, more children under the age of twelve received informal care by a grandparent than any other kind of care, formal or informal, while a profile of "American grandparents providing extensive child care to their grandchildren" published in 2001 showed that many adolescents, who don't exactly need care and probably wouldn't take it from any other source, welcome grandparents' caring companionship when parents are not around.

The particular importance of grandparents to teenage grandchildren is highlighted in a study of communication in British families. During the survey period, more than one in five of the teenagers who had spent time with a grandparent while their parents were at work had talked to that grandparent about personal issues and problems, including family breakdown, a higher proportion than had discussed such things with parents, teachers, or siblings.

Given the overwhelming importance of grandparents

> **Boy, aged thirteen**
> "Over the holidays Grammie and Gramps always say, 'Come by if you need anything,' and I do go by quite a lot. It's not exactly that I need anything— though Grandma's a stellar cook—it's that hanging out with them is a change from hanging out with my pals."

to many contemporary families, it is astonishing how little factual information we have about them. Even their identity is surrounded by question marks. It might seem that biology makes it perfectly clear who is and is not whose grandparent, but does it? If your child's grandmother is your husband's mother, she's your mother-in-law; if she's your mother, she's his mother-in-law, but what if

---

TWO GENERATIONS OF DIVORCE

*"Relationships between today's parents and grandparents are often
planted in yesterday's anxieties and misunderstandings, predating
the birth of the first grandchild. A divorce puts 'ex' in front of
most of those relationship names, and a remarriage introduces
the modern phenomenon of the stepgrandparent. And, of course,
a divorce may be followed by a new partnership that isn't a
marriage. Is the father of a parent's live-in lover her children's
grandfather—and if he is not so regarded now, how long must
the couple be together before he is? And what about the new
partner of the grandfather himself? Is she—or he—your children's
stepgrandmother or stepgrandfather even if the role has not been
formalized by law and the original partner is still around?"*

Source: Leach 2010a

---

she is his or your stepmother? One thing we do know is that not
all grandparents are loved and loving, and if yours are not, it is
very likely due to family breakdown in an earlier generation.

What we also know is that although studies involving extended
families do not always clearly distinguish between grandparents
and other relatives, between maternal and paternal grandparents,
or even between grandmothers and grandfathers, and while there
are certainly aunts, cousins, and step-everybodys who are lastingly important to children when immediate families break up,
the relatives who are likely to matter most, in every country, are maternal grandmothers: mothers' biological or
adoptive mothers and very occasionally stepmothers.

Unfortunately, parental separation does not always
bring grandparents closer to their children and grandchil-

**Mother of toddler, aged eighteen
months**

"I know they love him. And he loves
them, too. But taking him to see them
is really hard for me because they've
never really liked me, not from the first
time their son took me to a movie. They
didn't think I was good enough for him
then and now they're sure I'm not."

GRANDPARENTS IN SEPARATED FAMILIES

The Grandparents in Separated Families Study featured focus groups with fifty grandparents discussing their experience of the effects of parental separation on relationships with their grandchildren, their adult children, and their adult children's former partners. The findings provide insight into the causes and consequences of such issues as relocation and geographical distance, financial capacity, family relationships, moral judgments of right and wrong, commitment, use of legal processes and fairness, all of which appear to contribute to the growth or decline of post-separation relationships for grandparents.

Source: Deblaquiere, Moloney, and Weston 2012

dren. Sometimes that special relationship shrivels in the cold blast of family breakdown, with less and less contact between grandparents and grandchildren, not only while a separation or divorce is under way but forever after. Because it is the maternal grandmother, often supported by the maternal grandfather, who is most likely to be closely involved in supporting the separated family, and her support will be going to the mother and children, paternal grandparents are very vulnerable to gradual exclusion, and fathers are likely to be left without much support from their own parents. In research surveys, parents mostly say that it is important for children to have as much contact with both sets of grandparents after their parents are separated or divorced as they did before, but in real life that doesn't often happen. Many parents cannot help seeing the two older-generation households as enemy camps and cannot tolerate the idea of older children confiding private details of one parent's life to the parents of the other.

CURRENTLY, grandparents in the English-speaking world have no legal rights to see their grandchildren against the parents' wishes. In the United States, individual states vary in the details of their determination of grandparents' visitation rights:

VARIATION IN STATES' APPROACH TO GRANDPARENTS' VISITATION

California

Conditions for grandparent visitation rights include a determination of whether a parent is deceased, the child's parents are divorced or separated, the whereabouts of one parent is unknown, or the child is not residing with either parent. In addition to determining that visitation is in the child's best interests, the court must find that the grandparents had a pre-existing relationship with the grandchild. The court must also balance visitation with the parents' rights. If both parents agree that the court should not grant visitation to the grandchild, the court will presume that visitation is not in the child's best interests. Adoption does not automatically cut off the visitation rights of grandparents. Note that in 2001 a California Court of Appeals ruled that the state statute providing grandparental visitation was unconstitutional.

Florida

The Florida Supreme Court has ruled the Florida statute providing grandparental visitation unconstitutional, and the Florida Legislature has not adopted an alternative statute.

Georgia

The custody statute does not list specific factors for the court to consider for determining the best interest of the child. A court may award visitation rights if an action is pending where there is an issue involving the custody of a minor child, divorce of the child's parents, termination of a parent's rights, or visitation rights. Adoption cuts off the visitation rights of the grandparents unless the adoption is granted to a step-parent or a natural relative of the child.

Maine

A court may award visitation rights if at least one of the child's parents is deceased, visitation is thought to be in the child's best interest, and visitation will not interfere significantly with the relationship between the parent and the child. Adoption cuts off all visitation rights of grandparents.

Source: http://www.grandparents.com/family-and-relationships/
grandparents-rights/grandparent-rights-united-states

In the United Kingdom, grandparents whose children forbid contact with grandchildren can confidently go to the court for permission to apply for a contact order (see pp. 91–100). In the United States various organizations are campaigning with some success for grandparents to have legal rights to see their grandchildren irrespective of the parents' wishes. Such measures may help grandparents, but they do not seem likely to help the grandchildren.

Children can gain immeasurable support from grandparents who are closely and warmly involved with their separating parents as well as with them, but they are unlikely to find it helpful to have yet another adult fighting one or both parents for contact with them.

EXTENDED FAMILY AND OTHER SPECIAL ADULTS

When parents are behaving oddly it is helpful to children of all ages to have other adults around whom they know and trust and who are still behaving normally. Different adults may be special to different children: one child may hang on to a grandparent or caregiver; another may spend more and more time with the family of his best friend who lives close by, while it may be a teacher at school or college who is the most vital support for an older child or young adult.

Having your child strike up a close and confidential relationship with another adult—especially if it is not a family member—can leave you feeling hurt and anxious. Your child stays late after school several days a week or spends more and more time in another home, and gradually it becomes clear that he or she is doing so not just to spend time with a friend but also to spend time with one or other of the teachers or parents. Why will your child talk to that adult when he absolutely refuses to talk to you? Why will she take their advice and accept their comfort when she shrugs off yours? Try to understand that those adults are more acceptable and useful to your child right now precisely because they are *not* you. With the family collapsing around her, she is no longer sure what your values, judgments, and viewpoints are or whether she can go on assuming that what you do and say represents the adult world. She needs to find out whether other adults, especially adults she has sought out for herself, think and behave differently from you.

Such relationships with other parents, with teachers or any other caring adults, can be truly valuable to an adolescent. If you do find yourself enviously resenting them, remind yourself that the child is trying to understand what is happening in her family and her own feelings about it, and that if she cannot get sufficient help from family members, she is better off getting it from outside the family than not getting it at all. However, children who are unhappy and confused by what is going on at home are especially vulnerable to relationships with outsiders that cross the line from appropriate to inappropriate concern. If there is a special adult in your child's life and you find yourself anxious about the relationship, bringing it out into the open will be both helpful to your child and protective of her. If you and your ex agree to share at least an outline of what is going on with the child's chosen adult, your child will know that it's all right for her to confide in him or her if she wants to, and you can be confident that there is nothing secret in the adult's interest (see pp. 108–13). Of course it is right to be cautious, but remember that such an adult confidante is no more likely to treat your child irresponsibly than you would be if you were similarly placed with somebody else's child. One day perhaps you will be.

Most people that you tell about trouble in your family will inevitably take sides, of course. But if the two of you together confide in someone who is truly concerned for you all as a family, is espe-

> **Woman, now aged fifty**
>
> "I was twelve and at boarding school, extremely upset about what was going on at home, especially the brand-new stepmother who'd arrived in Dad's house. The school nurse caught me crying, and I confided this to her. Do you know what she said? She said, 'You're really lucky to have two mothers.'"

cially concerned for the children, and does you both the honor of assuming that they are your main concern, too, he or she may provide you all with emotional ballast during the stormiest times. Be careful whom you pick, though. Some people will make an enjoyable drama out of the sadness you are recounting, and enjoy passing it on, too. And an obtuse or insensitive adult can rip scabs off children instead of putting Band-Aids on.

IT'S NOT ONLY your children who need support: as you and your partner tear yourselves apart, you are both going to need other adults you can rely on. In theory, every nuclear family is the nucleus of an extended family. In practice, though, in our individualistic and mobile society, a nuclear family is often a more or less stand-alone unit consisting of a couple in a sexual partnership and children for whom they are solely responsible. That kind of family isn't the nucleus of anything, so instead of having support networks you can take for granted, you may have to work for them. Grandparents are an obvious starting point, but sadly, although many parents rely on grandparents for child care or babysitting if they happen to live nearby, as we have seen, not many intact couples regard the relationship between themselves and their own parents, or between grandparents and grandchildren, as highly important to family life. Few, for example, will turn down a change of job, or even of country, because it will take them much farther away.

> **Man, now aged thirty**
> "My mom's stepmother was really shocked when my mother left my father and moved in with another guy a bit younger than her. I was about ten, and I'd been told that they planned to marry and that my sisters and I could go and live with them. 'He may marry Emily,' said my grandmother, 'but there's no way he's going to take on all of you. Why would he?'"

If you are separating, you might regret having taken a cavalier approach to available grandparents—and even rethink it as you face up to the next stages of your family's life. Nuclear families are all very well as long as

Father of three daughters, aged two, six, and eight

"Her mom, dad, two aunts, and an uncle lived three doors down from us. I'd sometimes felt they were a bit too much in our faces, if you know what I mean, but when I moved out and moved away I realized just how important they were, and to me as well as to her.

"Her dad and her uncle were the people I had beers with. That held me together during the worst months before we separated, and not having that was one of the loneliest bits of living on my own. To my ex and the kids, their house was an extension of ours. I think it was the popping in and out that held her together, plus any or all of the women took care of Mandy so she had time to herself. Without it, she says, Mandy would have had a pretty boring six months and seen and heard a lot of crying and screaming. Kate liked to go and join in after school. She especially loved one of the aunts, who had lots of laughs for her at a time when her mom really didn't. And Jenny: well, being a bit older, I suppose, she worried about her mom and about me and about what was going to happen, and she took all that to her grandma . . ."

all's well, but if there is nothing and nobody to support them from outside, they are horribly vulnerable to disintegration if that central couple relationship goes wrong. It is when that is happening that the importance of extended family—or any other kind of support from outside—becomes painfully clear.

You obviously cannot invent loving relatives or even form friendship networks in the time it takes your marriage to break down, but do be aware of the importance of any you already have when you make decisions about separating and who is going to live where. One of you is going to be a lone parent and the other is going to be a mostly lone *person*. And for each of you "lone" will often mean lonely. The kind of support you most need may be mostly emotional, mostly practical, or both. People who love you and will always be there for you are a huge emotional resource wherever they live—even Paris, if you all use video chat. But people don't have to live halfway across the world to be too far away to be useful on a day-to-day basis.

Next-door neighbors whose children feel like your kids' cousins may be such an important asset (hopefully to both families)

that they are something to take into account when you're thinking about selling and moving. If you must move and can't stay
with the same neighbors, think about staying in the same neighborhood so that the children can at least stay at the same schools
with friends and familiar teachers, and you don't lose the friends
you have made at the school gate. School gate support networks
are a big part of daily life, especially while you have a child
at preschool or elementary school, but you may not want all of
them to know too much about your private affairs—which they
will if you tell any of them. If you must move right out of the
district to a new community, could you make a virtue out of
the necessity by moving close to the grandparents you've never
been able to see enough of, or even close to those old friends who
moved away last year?

PARENTS' LOVERS AND POTENTIAL PARTNERS

Parents separate for "grown-up" reasons and often because one
or both of them want a new and different "grown-up" life. Sometimes those reasons are clear fault lines in the original marriage,
such as one or both partners being abusive, alcoholic, or perhaps
addicted to drugs or gambling. But often those "grown-up" reasons have to do with having found, or being on the lookout for,
a new sexual partnership. When that's the case, it's especially
difficult to put children first.

If your marriage is falling apart primarily over an affair with
another man or woman, children will soon know, and if they
are old enough—over seven, say—to think about other people's
relationships at all, they will probably see the stranger as having
straightforwardly stolen one parent from the other. There is a
childish parallel in shifting best friendships at school, and children may find such a "theft" a more comprehensible—and even
more forgivable—reason for parents separating than the incom-
prehensible emotional betrayal of just not loving each other
anymore. But if children usually forgive the "stolen" parent-as-

victim, they may not easily forgive the person who "stole" him or her. If the love affair turns out to be a life affair, this can be a nightmarish route into step-parenting.

If another person comes on your scene after you have separated and new living arrangements have been achieved, do your ex the courtesy of telling him or her before anyone else does. Don't be in a hurry to tell your children, though, or to introduce him or her to them. They may deeply resent anyone who even appears to be edging into a missing parent's place, but that's the less dire of two equally probable possibilities. Children who have recently lost their taken-for-granted-everyday father are often easily enraptured by the making-an-effort charms of a new candidate. If he plays ball in the garden with the middle one, shoulders the littlest one on walks, talks usefully to the oldest about her forthcoming test, and makes you laugh, he may soon be a welcome visitor and within weeks an important part of the children's lives. If the two of you then decide that the relationship is not going anywhere—and face it, many affairs don't—childish hearts will be broken all over again, not because losing this man is as bad as losing their dad, but because losing their dad has left them acutely vulnerable to loss and the household short of an adult male. Although children react differently to changes to a household they visit rather than live in, roughly the same possibilities apply if the children's father introduces a new lover.

Research specifically on this point is rather sparse, but what there is strongly suggests that it's best to keep the new person merely as one of your friends in the children's eyes, and if your new lover also has children, the same will apply to him. Try to hold back any sense of the relationship being special and any business of the children's until you are truly convinced that it is going to be long-lasting and a partnership is planned between you and ready for implementation.

Until that time comes (if it ever does):

- Don't have a new sexual partner stay overnight with you when the children are in the house. Their reaction to finding you in bed or in the shower together will vary according to their ages, but every variation will be disastrous.

- Don't underestimate children's ability to pick up clues that this "friendship" is special. It doesn't take finding an intimate garment in the laundry basket to raise a child's suspicions; switching to the brand of tea he or she prefers or changing the newspaper you subscribe to may be enough.
- If the children live with you, don't encourage—or even allow—a new lover the privilege of parent-like behavior with your children, however tempting it may be to enlist his or her skills in making a birthday cake, picking up your daughter from a late party, or backing up your discipline.
- If the children live with your ex, don't try to squeeze in extra time with your lover by including him or her in the time you spend with your children. When they come to visit, they want to see you and only you, and they want to see you as you are with them not as you are with your new partner.
- Try not to change access arrangements simply in order to give yourself more child-free time to spend with this new person. If a month ago you didn't think your two-year-old was ready to sleep over with her father on weekends, she's very unlikely to be ready now.

If and when you are seriously contemplating making this relationship a partnership, if each of you has children and you are hoping to blend two single-parent households together, the relationships among the children will be almost as crucial to everyone's future happiness as the relationship between their parents. Take introductions slowly and listen to feelings carefully. There are stepbrothers and stepsisters who truly love one another, but you'll be lucky (and have done exceptionally well) if yours are among them.

If you want to try out the business of living together as a potential family group, try to do it on neutral territory rather than by inviting him or her to come and live with you and your children. If the money and the time can be afforded, a rented holiday home is often a good start. Nobody's territory is being invaded; nobody knows how to manage this environment, so everyone can work out the ground rules for living in it together.

Make sure your potential new partner realizes and accepts that your children already have two parents (even if they only see one at a time) and don't need another. Sometimes well-meaning people assume that lone parents want help with their parenting when what they really want help with is the lone bit. Make it clear that if all goes well, he or she can eventually become a highly significant adult in your children's lives but never their parent.

Beware of authority. Few children will readily accept instructions or reproofs from a comparative stranger, but many adults find it difficult to live with children without giving any. If your potential partner cannot manage this now, it is very likely to become a problem if you move in together or marry.

Beware of manipulation. Many children work hard to influence parents' choice of partner, usually in the direction of getting rid of anyone who threatens to move in. Techniques vary from the blatant (spiders in shoes) to the more subtle (pretend she isn't there at all). Either can be successfully off-putting.

Be sure it is understood that whatever the issue, you are and must be a parent first before you are a partner, and that as a parent you will be communicating with your ex and doing your best to maintain a cooperative—or at least polite—relationship.

CHILDREN'S STEP-PARENTS

Even if your child has known the soon-to-be step-parent for many months and really likes him or her, you may find that once he knows you plan an actual marriage his attitude changes for the worse. Perhaps the often extreme difficulties step-parents may have in relating to younger children start with ideas about them that children draw from fairy stories, in which step-parents of both sexes are invariably wicked and cruel. As for older children and teenagers, they might have replaced fairy-tale stereotypes with an awareness of the bad press given to step-parents, especially stepfathers, as perpetrators of child abuse.

Children can develop extremely close and warm relationships with step-parents. Some even maintain that despite the misery at the time, they are glad there was a divorce.

However, most children whose parents have divorced are not at all glad to have a step-parent. Many have found it impossible to accept that their parents' separation is permanent, and though the divorce has been finalized, they often go on for years dreaming of a reconciliation. Even for a child who really knows that a dream is only a dream and isn't going to happen, the idea of a parent marrying for

Girl, now aged sixteen

"I was twelve when they finally decided they wanted to get married, and I realized I was going to have a stepfather. I don't know what got into me, but I told a bunch of lies about him to my school friends—stupid things like he wore sandals with socks, which he never did—and to my grandma. I even told Grandma I didn't want to live with him and could I come and live with her. It's lucky I didn't make things up and tell them to my dad or it might really have caused trouble. But why did I tell my best friend I hated him? I liked him a lot and I'd known him for nearly two years as our closest family friend . . ."

Boy, aged twelve

"I'm closer to my stepdad than I've ever been or ever would have been to my real father. I just like him better. I think he's a much nicer man. And he makes my mom laugh. As to my littlest sister, she's three now, and I think she really feels like he's Daddy. She doesn't call him 'Daddy' 'cause Mom says things like, 'You've got one of those already,' but she calls him 'my-Da' in a cutesy sort of a voice. Mom thought I might mind, but I don't."

a second time finally moves those dream goalposts from improbable to impossible, and that's difficult to cope with.

Helping Children to Accept the Prospect and Reality of a Step-parent

Whether the new partner and the children concerned are yours, or you are the new partner and the children are his, the issues you are likely to face are the same. Although children survive the trauma of parental separation better if other aspects of life can stay the same (see above), the positive step of making a new family grouping usually goes more easily in a new environment. In these circumstances, a move to a different house often makes a better start than having all of you move in with him (or her) or vice versa. In a new home, everyone shares neutral territory about which nobody feels possessive, and there can be mutual ground rules for living in it from the beginning.

- Leaving room for the "real" parent is vital. That means room in the child's life—so that his regular visiting days and weekends with his other parent don't suddenly get lost in new-family activities—and psychological room, too. Don't expect him to call the step-parent "Mom" or "Dad," for example (unless he asks or does it spontaneously), or push him to make Mother's Day cards for the stepmother instead of, or even as well as, his biological mother.
- Try to make the new relationship completely extra to rather than instead of the original one. And make sure room is left for the original extended family, too. Encourage children's relationships with your ex's family and don't expect them to drop old family stories, in-jokes, and so forth. Tell them to the new person instead.
- Although their relationship is *because* of you, the step-parent and children cannot make it *through* you. Try not to stand in the middle, like a maypole around which everybody dances. Step-parent and children have to get to know one another as people rather than as your appendages. No matter how jealous a child may initially be of the newcomer, the chances are high that she

will enjoy your new happiness, give the step-parent credit for it, and eventually be ready to seek a share for herself.

- Don't expect the step-parent *or* children to accept gender-stereotyped family roles too quickly (if at all). A stepfather, for example, usually needs to go very easily on "discipline," "manners," and so forth. He may never be permitted an authoritative relationship with adolescents but may, if he will accept it, eventually be offered friendship instead. A stepmother will probably need to hold back on personal care, however warmly she feels toward the children. She may be felt to be "stepping beyond the bounds" if she tries to braid hair or wash necks, at least until the children spontaneously hug and kiss her.

- Try to arrange for the step-parent and natural parent to meet, especially if you have managed to keep your relationship civil since the divorce. Children need to feel that all the adults who are closely concerned with them are on the same side—their side. It also helps if they do not feel that they can easily play one off against the other or have their wilder fantasies taken seriously.

4

Practical and Legal Issues

A baby or toddler's environment and lifestyle is dominated by his relationships with the people he is attached to—principally his mother and then his father. But as he grows through toddlerhood and into a preschool child and then into a schoolchild, parents remain central, but other things come to matter, too. As you struggle with the sadness and the guilt of parental separation, you may find it comforting and helpful to realize how many practical aspects of your children's changing lives you can control and how much you can do to protect or rebuild their happiness and well-being.

The change from having both parents living with them in the same home to having the two of you living in separate places is one of the biggest a child can ever encounter. It is not just a storm but a hurricane that howls through family life, rocking all the relationships and wrecking children's security. You cannot avoid that change (if it were possible for you to stay together, no doubt you would be doing so), but parental separation tends to bring other changes along with it. Some of these you may be able to avoid, and if you can, you should. Moving to a new home, changing from one caregiver or preschool to another, or going to a new school are all normal life events that are stressful to most children even if they are securely embedded in intact families. But when normal events such as these are part of the abnormal disruption of the family caused by parental separation, they can be not just stressful but devastating. When family is in turmoil, the more smoothly the rest of their lives can carry on as before, the better children will cope. So before you plan on—or just accept—big changes like the ones dealt with in this chapter, make sure you ask yourselves—and each other—about other options. Above all, think geography.

FAMILY GEOGRAPHY AND CHILDREN'S SECURITY

Children's security depends on the people to whom they are attached being available. When parents separate, children lose the security of being able to take the presence of both of them together or either one of them at a time for granted. That's a huge loss, but just how acute and lasting it is largely depends on everybody's proximity. Daddy has left and that's scary, but where has he gone? The answer "into an apartment on the next block" is less scary than "the other side of town" and very, *very* much less scary than "a three-hour journey away," not to mention "to Australia," or, worst of all, "I don't know." Although everything that is most important and most difficult about making a separated family work for children depends primarily on parents maintaining a reasonable relationship with each other, staying within easy geographical reach is a close second—and the two often go together.

Avoiding the other big, stressful changes in children's lifestyle that will make parental separation harder to bear is also largely a matter of geography. If after Daddy leaves, you could find a way of staying in the same home, the children could then keep the bedrooms and the play space they are used to, keep the family cat or the beloved rabbits, ride the same bus to the same schools, and maintain their whole network of friends and neighbors, and so could you. Even if staying in the same house is financially impossible, the children could still keep the familiar infrastructure of their lives if you could find the smaller, cheaper home you need in the same neighborhood.

THE NEED FOR A HOME BASE

However many places there are where he spends time, a child must live somewhere, must have a home. A place and setting that we think of as "home" is highly important to most of us, but it may be especially so to children because they have so little control over their own lives and lack adults' nest-making experience and skills. If you move, temporarily or permanently, you will know where you are going—even if you go reluctantly—and whether it is into a new apartment, a hotel room, or a prison cell, you will at once settle down to making the new place feel as homelike as you can. A child doesn't move, he is moved; he has no idea where he is going or what it will be like. If the new place is stable and somebody helps him settle in it, he will eventually get past the fact that it is not home so that it can become so and give him back his security. But until or unless he has a home base, his life will lack stability.

Almost all children do move, of course; on average, families in the United States move four to six times while children are growing up. But most moves are job-related, are chosen (or at least accepted) by the parents, and maintain or even upgrade the family's standard of living. A move resulting from a family breakup is different; it is not something that both parents have chosen, indeed the loss of one parent is implicit in it, and as if that huge change in the family's lifestyle was not painful enough, the new place will usually be a step down. The contrast experienced by an eleven-year-old when she was moved from isolated countryside to an inner-city apartment was extreme (see facing page), and the whole experience was more shattering for her than the experiences of most children who move after parents part. However, it is salutary for parents to consider her devastation, because if her mother and father had been more aware of the particular issues that were critical to her, they could probably have managed to make a necessary move less traumatic.

Do arrange for the children and whichever parent is to live with them to stay in their existing home if that is at all possible, at least during the upheaval of the actual separation. They will get used to a home with only one parent in it a great deal more easily if the home *is* home. Changes within that home will probably be less disturbing than a move. A (carefully selected) lodger, for example, might make the

Woman, looking back to when she was eleven

"It wasn't just moving house; it was moving life. We'd lived deep in the country ever since I could remember (actually since I was three). I'd had a pony since I was seven. She was the center of everything I did and most of what I thought, too. Leaving her behind just felt like everything had come to an end. Like I had come to an end. And I didn't understand how to be in New York. How could you play with no garden and with people packed in on either side and above and below, hundreds of windows looking at you whenever you went out? Was I angry with them? No. I was too sad, too bewildered to be angry. I think I was grown-up and a parent myself before I could feel properly angry."

finances feasible without bothering children nearly as much as leaving the house. Be careful about doubling the children up so as to free a bedroom to rent out, though. Once children have had their own bedrooms, those separate rooms often become exceedingly important—perhaps especially to teenagers—and being suddenly forced to share can jeopardize sibling relationships just when they are at their most important.

If staying in the same home is impractical, try to look at the move from the children's points of view as far as practicalities allow. You may not be able to achieve what they want, but if you don't think about what it is that they want, you cannot even try. To your ten- to sixteen-year-old, a manageable journey to the same school and friendship group may be more important than any feature of the new home itself, while to younger children features of the new place, such as a garden or some outside play space, may be crucial, and anywhere that could not include the family cat or dog might be a disastrously poor choice.

Living in Two Places at Once

If the two of you share the care of your children after separation (see chapter 7), you may each want your place to be the one they think of as "home." Do be careful not to let that become one more of the many issues that your children feel they cannot even talk about for fear of hurting one of their parent's feelings. Adults squabbling over which place is home can make the children feel that neither place is, and that is a pity, because children need to live "at home" however much time they spend somewhere else.

For most children under the age of four or five, "home" will almost certainly be the place where Mom lives. If your children are past that stage, and one of you lives in the ex-family home or has a much more child-friendly place than the other, the question of which is "home" will settle itself. Likewise, if the children live almost full-time with whichever of you is resident parent, it is unlikely that the place where they visit the other parent—perhaps overnight every two weeks—will be labeled "home." However, if you are both fortunate enough to have places to live that the children like, especially if they are in the same neighborhood so that school and friends are accessible from either location, and the two of you are in civil contact with each other (see chapter 5), you may find that older children eventually come to regard both places in a similar way and the term "home" is dropped in favor of "Dad's" and "Mom's."

Even under those relatively benign circumstances, though, it isn't easy for a child to feel equally at home in two places. An adolescent might (theoretically at least) be able to decide spontaneously which home he's heading for on any particular day. If he decides to go to Dad's (because he'd like them to watch the soccer game together), all he has to do is call his mom to say he won't be there today, and his dad to say he will, then he should be good to go, able to let himself in and knowing that he'll find everything he needs where he left it. In the real world, though, people usually have to make plans and arrangements, if only so that somebody buys dinner and gets it eaten and nobody buys dinner and gets it wasted.

Whether you are trying to help your children feel that they have two homes as well as two parents, or arranging for smooth and enjoyable visits from your home to the other parent's, it helps to keep the business of transferring from one place to the other as simple as possible—though that may not be very easy.

- Cut down the amount of junk they need to think about, pack up, and carry back and forth with them in order to be comfortable in either house. Bathroom items, pj's, hairdryer, and an alarm clock can easily be duplicated. Clothes are more difficult. During the holidays, younger children may be fine for weekends as long as they have underwear and socks, a pair of sneakers, a set of old clothes to paint in,

  > **Girl, aged three**
  > "Why do my boots shrink at Daddy's house?"

  swimming gear, and maybe a raincoat. If it's a school day tomorrow, they'll need clean clothes. And keep checking everything for size.
- Maintaining clothing in two places for teenagers is much more difficult. It's most unlikely that the T-shirt they wore last time is still acceptable (let alone desirable) now, even if it has been washed. Adolescents want to wear the clothes they choose rather than the clothes that happen to be available, so the current selection will always have to go from one place to another.
- There are affordable ways of duplicating electronic equipment they can't do without. For instance, if younger children do not have or regularly carry their own laptops, make sure you have

the software they use for schoolwork and socializing on your computer and encourage them to carry their stuff back and forth on a memory stick or get comfortable accessing what they need from cloud storage. Many visits are ruined by lack of the right charger, so make sure they can charge phones and tablets (and whatever else they have) in either place.

- Leaving medical essentials behind can bring visits to a premature end. Make sure that medicines, daily-wear contact lenses, oral contraceptives, and so forth are duplicated. Remember to check use-by dates, especially on emergency-use items such as inhalers. A young person's general practitioner should be sympathetic to the need for extra prescriptions.
- If your children are to spend one or two days each week at the other parent's home, consider which days they should be not only from the adults' viewpoints but from the children's as well. If your cello-playing child has orchestra the day after her night at your house, the instrument has to go to school with her the day before. If after-school sports are mostly on Fridays, a tired, dirty child and all his gear will arrive late for the start of your precious weekend.

Don't feel that you have to try and make both places as like each other as possible. A four- or five-year-old may settle more easily if his bedding is familiar and the nightlight is "right," but as long as even slightly older children feel secure in the place they think of as "home" and are able to leave it and the resident parent easily, the fact that the other parent's place is different can be part of the pleasure of regular visits, in addition to the pleasure of spending time with him. Differences between the two homes can be part of the fun, giving children a bit of space in which to be different people. Different food, different music, different conversation, different games, and even some different ground rules can all be interesting extensions of life at home.

SCHOOLS

Sometimes parents forget how important school is to a child. The routines of going to school, the school's hours, the breaks, and the vacation dates are an important part of the structure of family life and will lend children stability during the upheavals of parental separation. But what actually goes on in school can strike parents as a mixture of mystery and trivia and something they don't have to think much about. Parents who are very much taken up with other things, such as problems between them and trying to work out how to manage a separation, are especially likely to take school for granted and think about the home child they see and know as if that was the whole child. It is not the whole child, of course. That same home child actually has to live those unseen hours, becoming a schoolchild for the whole of every day that the school is open and with no choice in the matter unless he convinces you that he is sick.

Folk wisdom says that "school days are the happiest days of your life." It's sad to think of an entire adult life offering no greater happiness than being a schoolchild, but if school days are not at least moderately and mostly happy, your child will be unhappy overall. He has to spend most of the waking hours of around 180 days of each year in school. It is not just a place where he goes to learn while his "real life" carries on at home. It is the place where he will have (or not have) most of his friends; where he will make (or not make) most of his meaningful relationships with nonfamily adults; where he will find (or fail to find) most of his sporting and leisure activities. School will, and should be, central to his life, so no parent is entitled to ignore what goes on there.

Getting Support from Schools

School may be especially important to children when parents are separating, because when things are in a muddle at home, school can provide much-needed structure and predictability, and being with peers may be truly supportive as well as a welcome distraction. If your very young child is liable to be tearful and visibly upset at school, it may be helpful to tell her teacher what is going on at home—or at least that something is—so that she can keep a sympathetic eye on her. An older child may not want anyone to know about your separation, and you should respect his or her confidence if you can. But if teachers express surprise because a previously cooperative student is being difficult, even aggressive, it is obviously better that they should know that he is under particular stresses so that any complaints about his behavior are dealt with as sympathetically as possible.

Sometimes it is not your child's behavior at school that causes anxiety but the difficulty in getting him there. Acute anxiety over going to school may be triggered by something that happened to you, not to him, and made him wonder if you were "all right." Sometimes the trigger is an obviously traumatic one, such as parents actually separating. But sometimes it is something more trivial. A minor depression, perhaps, which made the child aware that you were unhappy, or an overheard argument between you and his father, which made him wonder whether all was well between you or whether his family was going to break up.

Once a child is sensitized to your welfare and feels that he has to keep an eye out to be sure you are OK, being away at school all day can become intolerable because he imagines all the fearful things that may have happened to you while he was gone. Will you be there when he gets home? Will he find you crumpled in a pool of blood or in floods of tears? Will you have "gone crazy" so that you no longer know or love him? Once his imagination runs riot in this way, logical probabilities and possibilities cannot comfort him. The level of his anxiety will probably vary from day to day. At its worst, the anxiety may show up in physical symptoms such as stomach pains that make it impossible for him to eat breakfast, or headaches or migraines. When his anxiety level is very high, some or all of his typical physical symptoms may show up not only when he is actually faced with going to school but also when he is made to think about, or discuss, going to school.

That fear and fear-of-fear make a vicious circle. The child who finds himself upset on Monday mornings soon comes to dread those horrible feelings as well as the school that first evoked them (see pp. 172–83). Do go immediately to see whichever teacher is concerned with your child's well-being and enlist the school's help for him. Meanwhile, make sure that the child understands what is going on between you and his father, what is going to happen, and what you feel about it. The reality is sad, but it is nowhere near as terrifying as those fantasies. Between your efforts and those of a sympathetic teacher, he may be able to cope, but if having someone else to talk to would make it easier, you can probably enlist further help from the school psychological service available in your district.

Changing Schools

Going to a new school is a big and important change for most children. Over the years, they will make several school changes as part of the public school systems of different countries. In the United States, children in all states begin compulsory and free education in kindergarten at five years, then move into elementary school, ages six to eleven, followed by middle school from eleven to fourteen, and then high school from fourteen to eighteen. Those regular moves are recognized as stressful for children, not only because new institutions with their different organizational structures and demands are always daunting but also because leaving the school a child is settled in always involves losing some important relationships that have to be replaced in the new one.

Children who move at the expected transition times and within the same community will usually find themselves moving up the system with at least some classmates and into a school that knows where they have come from and has probably put a lot of thought into its "transition arrangements." The children who are likely to find a move really difficult are the ones who move from one school to another outside those expected times, especially if they move midyear and perhaps to a different part of the state. If your child is midway through grade school or is in the second year of middle school, you obviously cannot wait to move him until he reaches the next conventional moving age. But you may be able to wait to move him until the end of the current school year just by delaying your house sale or purchase so the whole deal takes an extra couple of months. If you find the idea of "going slow" acceptable and it is unlikely to pose a risk to the final deal, it may be worth doing.

Part of the importance of the relationships children make in school and the activities they take up is that these things are separate from you and from home. You cannot do this for him in the new school (as you may have done in preschool), but you may be able to help him do it for himself. Whatever the age of the child, though, in a parent's dealings with a school, there is always a fine line to be drawn between interference and neglect. The happy medium has something to do with always being interested enough to listen and a lot to do with always being willing, even eager, to be involved whenever the child

---

THE COSTS AND BENEFITS OF CHANGING SCHOOLS

Many children in the United States change schools more often than the built-in transition from elementary to middle school. In Texas public schools, for example, one-third of all children change schools between fourth and seventh grades. The outcome of such moves depends largely on their intention. Moves that are instigated by parents seeking a better school for their children may lead to academic improvement. Moves dictated by divorce, job loss, or other family problems commonly disrupt children's academic progress.

Source: Hanushek, Kain, and Rivkin 2004

---

or the school issues any kind of invitation. When your child is starting at a school where he knows nobody and is the only one who is new, a bit of extra parental participation will certainly help, but what will help most of all is your awareness of what he is up against and your ability to sense when he is struggling and wants your support, and when he is managing himself and wants to live his school life without any parental involvement at all.

As well as being immediately stressful for children, extra and ill-timed school moves may reduce school performance.

Apart from stress-related problems, including anxiety over leaving home (see chapter 8), there seem to be two main reasons why children's education suffers from changing schools midyear or in years other than the conventional ones. First, these children are often moved from one school to another because their families can no longer afford to continue living where they are. When a family moves to a less expensive area or seeks cheaper housing some distance away, the family will probably move into a new school district where schools as a whole are likely to be less well funded and are lower-performing. Depending on the policies of the school board representing the new community, new arrivals, especially those arriving midyear, may have little choice among those local schools because there is pressure for space in the more desirable schools and unfilled space in the less desirable. Second, moving schools may mean that a child misses substantial chunks of schooling. In some states and school districts, there may be considerable delays in admission. So, however hard you try to work with the system, and however flexible you are prepared to be about the distance your child travels from a new home to a new school, that child may nevertheless find himself without any school place for many weeks and then in a school that you would never have chosen for him. If his schoolwork was already suffering in reaction to the family breakdown (see chapter 2), what should have been a temporary dip in his educational attainment may become a lasting drop.

MONEY MATTERS

Parents' ability to keep the practical aspects of family life running smoothly while the emotional part is struggling unfortunately depends largely on money. Don't underestimate the costs of getting a divorce in the first place. In the United States costs vary from state to state but average around $15,000. If the two of you cannot work out the terms of your divorce between you and lawyers have to be enlisted, the costs of your divorce will soar and so will its emotional costs to your children. The more you fight, the more they will suffer.

As we have seen (see introduction), people who are well-off are less likely to get divorced in the first place, but if they do split up, a good income certainly helps to dress everybody's wounds. However comfortably off you may be when your separation becomes inevitable, though, it is likely that you will be very much poorer by the time things settle down.

- The resources that have supported one home and family will have to support one and a half and probably eventually two.
- Some expensive possessions may have to be doubled up—the car, for instance.
- Resources may dwindle if, for example, it is impossible for both of you to go on working full-time because child care arrangements that formerly made it possible (such as a nanny or a full-time day care) are no longer affordable.
- If the resident parent and the children move out of the neighborhood, child care that was available without cost from grandparents or friends may be out of geographical reach.
- If the other parent moves out of the district, staying in contact with the children will depend on there being money for travel.

Child Support

"Child support" is the term used for financial support that helps toward a child's everyday living costs. Child support is for children under sixteen or under twenty for children in full-time education. It is paid by the parent who doesn't have day-to-day care of the child (the "paying parent") to the parent or person such as a grandparent or guardian who does (the "receiving parent"). There are statutory services (the Office of Child Support Enforcement) that will work out how much ought to be paid in your particular circumstances and will, in theory at least, collect it for you.

Service is provided by—and varies between—states. Many of those who seek help from the statutory bodies will have to pay toward the service.

Unfortunately, these services are not always as good as they sound. Unless your ex voluntarily pays regular child support directly to you, don't overestimate the financial help this source will provide for caring for your children after you have

---

TYPES OF HELP AVAILABLE FROM STATUTORY CHILD SUPPORT SERVICES

These services can help you to:

- Find the other parent if you do not have an address.
- Sort out any issues concerning parentage, arranging DNA testing if necessary. Work out how much child support should be paid.
- Arrange for the "paying parent" to pay child support.
- Pass payments on to the "receiving parent."
- Look at the payments again when either parent reports changes in their circumstances.
- Take action if payments are not made, including having the employer withhold money from the paying parent's paycheck or benefits.

Source: http://www.acf.hhs.gov/programs/ass/statesystems

SINGLE-PARENT FAMILIES AND POVERTY IN THE UNITED STATES

For the first time in history, children are more likely to reside in a single-parent family for reasons other than the death of a parent. Ninety percent of single-parent families are headed by females. Single mothers with dependent children have the highest rate of poverty across all demographic groups. Approximately 60 percent of American children living in mother-only families are impoverished, compared with only 11 percent of two-parent families. The rate of poverty is even higher in African American single-parent families, in which two out of every three children are poor.

Effects of Single-Parent Upbringing on Children

Children from single-parent families have increased risks to psychological development, social behavior, and sex-role identification and are more likely to drop out of school, bear children out of wedlock, and have trouble keeping jobs as young adults. However, many of these findings came from studies that adopted a "deviant" model of single-family structures. It is now accepted that confounding variables, such as income and social class, explain most of the negative findings. Lack of income has been identified as the single most important factor in accounting for the differences in children from various family forms.

Poverty

The median annual income for female-headed households with children under six years old is roughly one-fourth that of two-parent families, although the number of children per family unit is generally comparable (two per household).

Mother-only families are more likely to be poor because of:

- The lower earning capacity of women. Approximately 53 percent of single mothers are not in the workforce because they are unable to find affordable, quality child care. The majority of these mothers have no high school diploma, leaving them with few job opportunities or jobs that pay only the minimum wage.

- Inadequate public assistance.
- Lack of child care subsidies. On average, a poor mother spends 32 percent of her total weekly income on child care. This percentage nearly doubles when more than one child needs care.
- Lack of enforced child support from nonresidential fathers.

African American single mothers and their children may experience the most adverse consequences of unemployment because their earnings constitute a greater percentage of their total family income. The reasons cited for this disparity are that African American mothers are less likely to be awarded child support payments, to receive child support payments, or to have a second wage earner living in the household.

Adaptive Single-Parent Families

Despite the seemingly insurmountable challenges facing poor single parents, many are able to function well and to promote education, resourcefulness, and responsibility in their children. Successful single-parent families have adopted more adaptive functioning styles including:

- More available personal resources, which enhances their coping effectiveness.
- Better family organization, which balances household responsibilities and decreases task overload.
- A positive family concept, which values loyalty, home centeredness, consideration, communication, and closeness.
- An ability to highlight positive events and place less emphasis on negative aspects of stressful events.
- Possessing less stress-producing, more supportive social networks.

Source: Kirby 2012

separated. The more you and your children need the money, and the more you have had to use welfare assistance while waiting for it, the less likely you are to receive all, or indeed any, of it. A 2007 study conducted through the University of Baltimore estimates that in the United States as a whole, 50 percent of all child support arrears are owed to the government to reimburse welfare expenses. Half of the states pass along none of the child support they collect to low-income families receiving welfare and other assistance, instead reimbursing themselves and the federal government. Most of the other states pass along only $50 per month.

In many states "noncompliant" parents, who refuse or avoid support payments, may be subject to a large range of draconian enforcement measures, which vary by jurisdiction, the length of time the parent has been noncompliant, and the amount owed. Typical penalties include wage garnishment and denial or suspension of driver's, hunting, and professional licenses. Noncompliant parents who are more than $2,500 in arrears may be denied passports under the Passport Denial Program. Furthermore, nonpayment of child support may be treated as a criminal offense or a civil offense, and it can result in a prison or jail term. In New York, for example, continuous failure to provide child support is a Class E felony punishable by up to four years in prison. On any day in the current year it is estimated that roughly fifty thousand individuals are incarcerated in U.S. jails and prisons as a result of child-support debts. In addition, child-support debtors are subject to fines and property seizure.

When resident parents receive less support than their calculated entitlement, it is not always because their ex-partners refuse to pay what they owe or because agencies fail to take action to ensure payment. Sometimes it is because the agency's original calculations of what should be paid were incorrect. There are many unfortunate fathers who, having made regular payments of exactly what they were told they owed, suddenly hear that the level of payment was inadequate from the beginning, and they now face accumulated arrears. To avoid this, it is probably wise to check the claim made on you for child maintenance using one of several do-it-yourself calculators available on the Internet. If the claim seems low, don't gratefully assume that it is correct; query it with the agency or your lawyer.

Some parents are surprised to discover that child support and visitation are not legally connected. Many fathers feel that paying support gives them the right to see the children. In fact the only "rights" involved are the children's right to see their fathers whether they pay maintenance or not. Likewise, many mothers whose exes do not pay the support that is due from them are taken aback when they find that they cannot use nonpayment as a reason to deny or limit fathers' access or use the threat of denying access to force them to pay. The vital point for both parents to remember is that children are the subjects rather than the objects of both child support money and access visits. The money is not paid by the father to the mother for *her* benefit but for the child's. And access visits are not a father's privilege, which he must earn or can lose, or a mother's gift, but a child's right.

LEGAL ISSUES

Couples seeking a legal termination of their marriage—divorce or dissolution—must obtain a judicial decree from their state's court that the marriage is dissolved. Only after a divorce has been legally finalized in that way are the now-ex-husband and -wife free to remarry.

The content of divorce orders varies according to the specific circumstances, such as whether there are children to be provided for or property to be divided. These orders may therefore deal with matters such as property and bill division, alimony or spousal support, child custody, visitation, and child support, as well as any other pertinent matters that the court judges to be necessary.

A divorce action may be initiated by one party or both parties and may be contested or uncontested. When both spouses want—or at least accept—the divorce and come to an agreement on any relevant issues, they may obtain an uncontested divorce, which goes relatively quickly through the court process and may often be obtained without legal counsel and its associated expense. Most divorces are uncontested.

A SMALLER GROUP of married couples, though, are unable or unwilling to agree to the termination of their marriage or to its terms or are unable to settle the ensuing issues. Divorces that are contested take a great deal longer and, because it is necessary to retain legal counsel, are usually relatively costly. Even after issues have been agreed, judicial intervention will be needed to obtain legally binding orders.

Like marriage, divorce in the United States is the province of state governments, not the federal government, and divorce laws, policies, and procedures often vary greatly from one state to the next. For example, although by 2010 all states had allowed "no fault" divorce proceedings—on grounds such as "irreconcilable differences," "irretrievable breakdown of the marriage," "incompatibility," or a period of living apart—courts in many states still take the behavior of the individuals concerned into account when dividing up property or debts or evaluating custody, and some states require a period of legal and/or physical separation prior to granting a formal divorce decree.

Where divorce involves children, there is always a risk that the dispute between divorcing parents will spill over into a child custody case in court. Governments strive to prevent this use of extra resources, and all states now require parents to file a parenting plan or to decide where (and with whom) the children will live, how much access to them the nonresident parent will have, and who will pay for their support before divorces can be finalized. Details of custody and visitation can be filed in a written agreement between the parties or determined in a court hearing.

Seeking Mediation

If you are both willing to try to come to an agreement but find it impossible to make plans together that will really stick, mediation may help. Mediation is not legal advice (although a court may instruct you to seek it), and it is not counseling; it is designed to help people sort out their differences for themselves and reach genuine agreement. Mediation will not focus on resolving emotional issues or relationship breakdown but on practical matters. The mediator, who will neither take sides nor tell you what to do, meets with the two of you, usually for several sessions, and encourages you to set out your disagreements openly and honestly and resolve them yourselves. Mediation seldom works unless both of you genuinely want to reach agreement; but provided you do, it is often effective even if your views were far apart at the beginning. Mediation is not free, but it is usually considerably less expensive than taking advice from a traditional legal representative; make sure you ask about costs before you begin. Mediated settlements are often approved relatively quickly by the courts.

Collaborative Law

If an impartial mediator cannot help you to reach joint decisions, especially if you feel that you are being bullied or threatened to make an "agreement" you don't want to accept, you may need a lawyer to help you negotiate, and if one of you has a lawyer, the other parent will need to have his or her own. Choose carefully, though. Some people report that the involvement of legal professionals and the courts contributed more to chaos than to calm in children's lives. Certainly the adversarial system lawyers represent and work within can make for an atmosphere of unrelenting hostility, even aggression, between separating parents, so that even if you are trying to cooperate for the children's good, their involvement makes that more difficult. Around the courts and the offices of legal professionals, it sometimes seems that there is more discussion of what is fair to women and to men than there is about what will be best for individual children. When it comes to children's living arrangements and to access for the nonresident parent, you may be the only ones paying attention to what will work for younger children or being prepared to listen to what older children want.

Attorneys who practice "collaborative" law are committed to negotiating a settlement without engaging in litigation. You and your ex-partner discuss your differences face-to-face, as you might in mediation, but with the important difference that each of you has your own attorney present at each meeting. Unlike a mediator, each attorney will provide his or her client with support and advice and perhaps the services of neutral specialists in relevant matters such as finance or family dynamics, but unlike traditional practice in which lawyers work against each other, they will work together in the interests of helping the couple reach mutual agreements. If the collaborative process ends without the two of you reaching agreement and a planned settlement, the lawyers who have been involved cannot take the case any further. They are disqualified and must be replaced by new attorneys.

When you have found a lawyer you find sympathetic, make sure you understand the likely costs before you ask him or her to act on your behalf. Some lawyers (including some practicing collaborative law) offer "fixed fee family law services," in which the costs of each stage of your case are laid down in advance. This makes it much easier to budget. Without such an arrangement, costs that accumulate outside office visits—for phone calls, for example, or for photocopying and posting documents to your ex's lawyer—can be unexpected and surprisingly high. Unlike a mediator, a lawyer who is not practicing collaborative law will be on the side of the person who employs him or her (which is why each of you may want to employ your own). It is the individual who sought the consultation and will pay the bill whose rights and options will be addressed. When you have decided which of these options you want to pursue, your lawyer will negotiate on your behalf with your ex's lawyer, probably by making phone calls and writing letters.

Whether you and your partner iron out your disagreements between yourselves or with the help of a mediator or an attorney, your agreement will only be legally binding once it has been drafted by an attorney and signed by both of you with whatever particular formality is required by your state. This document confirms your detailed agreement concerning financial affairs, property, and child support. The court will usually demand to see this agreement before granting a divorce, but do make sure that the court has ratified it. There have been cases in which agreements were left in draft, which allowed them to be readdressed by one of the parties who, sometimes years later, saw a possibility of improving his or her settlement.

If Negotiation Fails: Asking or Allowing the Court to Decide

If you and your ex cannot agree on arrangements for your children even after a mediator or lawyers working collaboratively have tried to help you, you may have to apply to the court to decide between you on the outstanding matters. You should be aware that this is a last resort and likely to be highly stressful if you represent yourself and very expensive if you seek legal representation.

The main reason you start divorce proceedings is to end your marriage; divorce cannot be granted until its terms have been settled, so if you and your ex have been unable to reach agreement, the judge will decide between you, especially on issues involving children, property, and finances.

In a small minority of cases, aspects of a disputed divorce settlement will reach family court. Divorces cannot be granted in family court, but family court judges hear many cases that are related to parental separation and divorce, including child protection issues, child custody, visitation, and support, domestic violence, guardianship, paternity, and persons in need of supervision (PINS).

The details of which court hears which case under what circumstances are complex and vary widely from state to state.

It is essential that you seek information for the state in which you live. In New York State, for example, if parents are already involved in a divorce case in the supreme court, a request for child support or spousal support should be made there so that all the issues can be heard together. However, a married person seeking spousal support may file a petition in family court, and a divorced person can ask family court to modify an existing order of support, but a divorced person seeking a new order of spousal support cannot do that in family court but must go instead to the supreme court.

Custody and Visitation

Both parents have a legal right to ask for custody and visitation in a divorce proceeding. Apart from financial matters, these linked issues are the cause of most divorce court battles.

Custody is a parent's legal right to control his or her child's upbringing. It may also be referred to as "parenting." Custody has two parts: legal and physical. Legal custody is the right to make major decisions about your child, including where your child goes to school, what kind of religious training he or she receives, and whether or not your child gets surgery. Physical custody is the right to be the person the child lives with on a day-to-day basis. A parent with primary physical custody is sometimes called the "custodial parent" or the child's "primary caretaker." Joint custody gives both parents both elements of custody in equal measure.

Visitation is also known as "spending time with the child(ren)." A parent who does not have legal custody will still likely be entitled to visitation.

You can apply for a single court order, or a number of them, depending on which issues remain outstanding between the two of you. Where children are concerned, the court will make a particular order if, and only if, it considers that the results of the order would be better for the child than the status quo, and this is usually the case. Bear in mind, though, that the terms of the order you get may not be the terms you hoped for or the terms

HOW A JUDGE DECIDES CUSTODY

When determining custody and visitation, a judge will consider what is in the best interests of the child(ren). Some factors a judge may consider include:

- Who has been the child's primary caretaker.
- The quality of each parent's home environment.
- How "fit" the judge thinks each parent is (stable home and lifestyle, good judgment, steady employment, good mental and physical health).
- Which parent the child is living with now and over what period.
- Each parent's ability to provide emotional and intellectual support for the child.
- Which parent allows the other parent into the child's life (does not try to cut out the other parent or alienate the child from him or her).
- Which parent the child wants to live with (if the child is old enough to express a view and have it listened to).
- Whether a proposed custody arrangement would separate the child from any siblings.
- Whether either parent has been abusive.

A judge must consider whether there has been domestic violence.

Source: CourtHelp, LawHelp.org

you had expected based on the experience of divorced friends from out of state. Once you have applied to the court in this way, it will do what it considers best for the child.

A child's mother, father, or anyone with parental responsibility can apply for a court order. Other people, such as grandparents, can also apply for these court orders if they first get permission from the court.

Making an Application to the Court

Whoever is making the application to the court must complete a form stating the reason for the application. The court will set a date for the application to be heard.

The First Hearing

Usually, parents, their legal advisers, and a judge will attend the first hearing. Any particular problems will be discussed, and the judge may try to reach a quick agreement. If an agreement is reached at the first hearing, the court can decide whether to make an order immediately, confirming arrangements.

After the First Hearing

If an agreement has not been reached at the first hearing, the court may require you both to attend a meeting about mediation or a separated parents information program.

The court may decide to arrange another hearing for a later date, allowing time for more evidence to be gathered and a report prepared. It may take six to twelve months for the court to reach decisions about financial matters.

The court orders that are concerned with children are the most difficult, complex, and, arguably, most important. They are also especially widely variable from state to state as the contrast between New York State and Florida shows.

In New York (and many other states) these orders are labeled "Custody and Visitation." Both parents have a legal right to ask for custody and visitation in a divorce proceeding.

In some states, notably Florida (as of fall 2009), the terms "custody" and "visitation" have fallen out of use. Instead, the law requires a "parenting plan" for the children, and if the parents cannot agree on one, the court must develop a plan that includes a detailed schedule allocating the time the children will spend with each parent. Additionally, this plan needs to include an outline of which parent will be responsible for many parenting activities including:

- Daily tasks
- Health care
- School functions
- Holiday arrangements

- Extracurricular activities
- Communication with the children

In creating this parenting plan, the court is always guided by the best interests of the children and not by the needs and/or wants of the parent. The law recognizes that both parents have equal rights to spend time with the children, and the former presumption that mothers should have "custody" of the children, especially when they were young, has been abolished in favor of the legal requirement that the court consider a number of factors including:

- Length of time the child has lived in a stable environment and the desire to maintain continuity
- Moral fitness, mental health, and physical health of the parents
- The ability of each parent to maintain a stable routine for the child
- The presence of domestic violence
- The ability of each parent to meet the developmental needs of the child
- The likelihood of each parent permitting, and not interfering with, the contact and access rights of the other parent

THERE ARE MANY other facets and factors to consider when planning for the care and lifestyle of a child after parental separation or divorce. The court may ask for specialist assistance, such as an assessment of the family dynamics and the children's relationships with each parent, by a psychologist or other expert witness, but even added professional input cannot compensate for the court's lack of personal knowledge of the child for whom it is making such vital judgments. If it is possible for parents to resolve issues of this kind by agreement, it is highly likely that the judge will approve the order you ask for.

Enforcing Court Orders

If you disagree with the terms of a court order, you may be able to appeal against it. Appealing is difficult and complicated, and you will need legal advice, which will be expensive. However, appealing against an order is definitely preferable to ignoring or breaching it.

PART II

Separating Better—or Worse

5

Keeping Parenting and Partnership Apart

There are almost as many ways of coping or failing to cope with parental separation and divorce as there are parents separating, and no book can sensibly suggest which will feel best, or least horrible, to you. However, it does seem that from the point of view of children—children in general, not specifically yours—there are better and worse ways of handling it, emotionally and practically. All the positive ways go together and so do all the negative ways. If (almost) everything you say and do for your children, and the arrangements you make for them, now and months or years ahead, fit with the better group, you're making good choices. If a lot of it fits under worse, you're not.

THE VERY BEST WAY to manage the breakup of a family with minimal long-term harm to children is to be determined to support the relationships each of you has with each of your children and to protect them from the failure of the relationship between the two of you. That's not an easy thing to do, and if you are a mother (or father) reading this when you are almost overwhelmed with hurt and fury at the children's father (or mother), it may seem downright impossible. Some people do manage it, though, and it is the most important effort you can make for your children right now because it will affect every aspect of their lives both during and after your separation and divorce.

Whatever you are feeling about your soon-to-be-ex as a husband or partner, it is, and should be, irrelevant to what your children feel about him as their father. He's never going to be "ex" to them (the two of you may be getting divorced, but he's not divorcing the children). And even if you think he stinks as a dad, your children don't. To them he's just Daddy. He's the only father they know, and, bitter though it may be for you to acknowledge it right now, they love him as they love you. Each child has two beloved parents. You're going to be a lone parent, but that need not and should not mean that your children are going to be motherless or fatherless.

Feeling motherless or fatherless is terrible for a child of any age (see chapter 1), but watching a parent struggling with the sadness, anger, and depression of separation is also miserable for a child. Many people believe that children don't notice or care what is happening to adults, that they are only concerned with their own feelings and aren't even aware of anyone else's. That is a misapprehension and an important one. When children behave in ways that seem thoughtless, it is often because of their immaturity. Young children don't continue playing noisy games when you've told them you have a headache because they don't care about you but because they haven't yet developed the empathy that lets them put themselves in your shoes and realize that lots of noise will make your headache worse. With any luck, they don't even really know what "headache" means. As children get older, their seemingly endless demands for your attention, even when you are on the phone or watching something on TV, are not because they are spoiled and care only about themselves but because you are so much the center of their lives that they find it hard to believe that they are not the entire center of yours.

Children of all ages are extremely sensitive to parents' moods and feelings. The cues a baby uses are not the same as an older child's, of course, and the understanding a four-year-old brings to what is going on is not the same as an adolescent's; but whatever his age, your child will sense when either or both of you are unhappy and distracted or irritated and enraged with each other and will worry about you both. Just as bereaved children mourn differently than adults and are sometimes thought to be heartless, children show this kind of worry in different ways from adults. Your son is as likely to bring you an extra-large beetle to stroke as to stroke your arm. But however childish concern is expressed, it's important to recognize it so that you do what you can to reassure children that you are basically OK. You won't be able to conceal your feelings altogether. And you can't reassure children by trying to pretend that everything about the family is fine when it is not; nothing will confuse them more than having you tell them one thing when they clearly sense another. So, while trying to keep household routines ordinary and taking the trouble not to say nasty disparaging things about each other within a child's hearing (on the phone or to a friend as well as face-to-face) will be a good start, it isn't enough.

To make the best of what is inevitably a bad situation for the child, each of you needs to make a clear separation in your mind and in your behavior between the adult-to-adult and the adult-to-child relationships in the family. Keeping partner and parent relationships separate means that when you are with a child you won't say (or even let your face betray) the hurt, angry feelings that belong to your marital relationship as woman to man but don't belong to your son or daughter's relationship as child to father. If (and when) you can manage that, your child will know that the unhappiness she sees and senses is only adult business; the parenting business that is central to her life is still intact.

The quote from the father of the four-year-old girl (see next page) makes it tragically clear that he has *not* managed to separate his relationship with his wife from his child's relationship with her. At that point in the family upheaval, he felt that he

Father of girl, aged four
"Yes, I know she loves her, too. And Izzie loves her mom, come to that. But she can't love her the way I do or she wouldn't have walked out, would she? They say it's really rare for mothers to split, and if one parent walks out, it's usually the dad, but I'd never, never have done that. Never."

Mother of girl, aged five
"We both love her to death. Always have. Always will, I guess. But we couldn't go on living and fighting together, and if one of us had to move out, it was better for Emily that it was him."

and his little daughter had been equally "left" and that the loss of love for himself that led to the separation included the child. "She can't love her the way I do" is not a good starting point for mutual parenting.

In contrast, see the quote from the mother of the five-year-old girl (at left). Even those few words suggest a fundamental difference between the relationships of the two couples. The father feels that he and his little daughter are both victims in the separation: both were abandoned. The mother, on the other hand, sees the marital breakup as separate business and the father leaving the family home as the next step, which both parents thought best for the child.

Keeping parenting apart from partnership is somewhat easier when you realize that children, whatever their ages, don't want to share or even hear about their parents' man-to-woman relationships. They may love to hear stories about how you met or the drive to the hospital the night they were born, but they will resist and resent being made to recognize and think about your emotional and especially your sexual lives with each other. That relationship is adult business, not children's. The feelings that go with a dissolving marriage are not something they are ready for themselves and hearing too much about it can splash embarrassment around the parental relationships also. Using a child as a confidante is at best inappropriate, at worst sometimes close to abusive.

THE DISINTEGRATION OF your marriage or committed partnership will certainly be bad for your children whatever you do, but if you want to protect them from the very worst of it, you'll both do all you can to keep your hurt, sense of betrayal, loneliness, and fury private from them and keep the arguments and fights that belong to your adult and sexual relationship, not to their child-to-parent relationships, as quiet as you can.

Almost as difficult and even more important, you'll struggle to prevent what you feel about the person who broke up your partnership from changing what you've always felt about him or her as a parent. If the man who has left you was an OK dad before your adult relationship blew up, he still will be if circumstances (and you) allow him. If he's always been an active parent, loving and hands-on, you need to manage to go on believing in his absolute reliability as a father, respecting his input into every aspect of the child's upbringing and

Girl, aged twelve
"When we were at his house, Dad did talk—would talk—about him and Mom and how much he missed her and how she'd betrayed him. It didn't make me sorry for him. It made me embarrassed, especially when it looked as if he was going to cry. One time he'd been drinking bourbon and he got all emotional and started talking about getting lonely for her in bed. Yuck. That put me off both of them."

Mother of two boys, aged four and eight
"His second affair threw up a lot of shit between us, but even before it had settled I realized that he was still the only person in the world I could trust with the boys, the only person who'd drop everything for them in any kind of emergency and handle it, whatever it was, just the way I'd want. I had other people supporting me as a lone mom, but I'd think about dying, and what would happen to Luke and Larry if I did, and the thought of them going to live with their grandmother or one of their aunts gave me the absolute shudders. Their father is the only other person they 100 percent love and who would bring them up the way we'd planned. So I didn't want him for me—let's face it, didn't want him in my bed anymore— but I did want him for our children and that's dictated all our arrangements ever since."

enjoying their pleasure in each other. It isn't easy, but it is possible, especially if both of you feel at least some degree of joint responsibility for the separation and if there isn't a third party closely involved. It's difficult enough to be positive about your child spending the weekend with the other parent, much more difficult if there's a substitute-you there, too (see pp. 67–73).

When separating parents do manage to salvage intact not only their own but each other's parenting, they sometimes find that part of the lonely space left by the broken partnership has been filled with mutual parenting. That's the best possible gift they can make to their children.

MUTUAL PARENTING

Mutual parenting is not at all the same as shared or equal parenting. Those terms usually refer to arrangements in which a child's time (and therefore care) is shared between mother and father and is dealt with in chapter 7.

Father of girl, aged two during the divorce and now aged five
"If Diane had been older, maybe we'd have tried separate homes close by so she could pop in and out. But with her so little, we weren't going to divide her up, so we divided ourselves up: split the house into two apartments. We have half each; she has it all. Lots of people, like neighbors who aren't real friends, don't even realize we're divorced. Diane knows of course, but it really doesn't bother her. Why should it? There's always a parent at home, and there's always dinner in one of two kitchens, and her own precious bed."

Mutual parenting means that whatever else is or is not going on in your relationship with each other—today, this month, or next year—you are jointly committed to putting your children's well-being and happiness first and to protecting them as far as you can from any ill effects following your separation. The most important word in that sentence is "jointly." Many separating mothers say that they put their children first, and many fathers say that they do, too, but not many of them credit each other with doing so or manage to do it together.

The most difficult aspect of making your children's well-being a mutual priority is that it involves you two being together, or at least in frequent communication, when you'd probably prefer to have nothing whatsoever to do with each other. What is more, if you are very bitter toward your ex, you may find that although you are sure of your own commitment and good intentions toward the children, you struggle to believe in those of a person you are currently finding it impossible to tolerate or trust, let alone like. It is a worthwhile struggle, though, because conflict between the parents is known to be the very worst aspect of many children's experience of family breakdown: they suffer far more from your enmity than from the actual separation.

Even leaving aside the stress of having to be in touch with an ex-partner, putting children first doesn't come easily to all separating parents—or to all parents in intact families, for that matter. Seeing divorce as the way out of a marriage that's become miserable, some feel that they are entitled to make seeking their own happiness their priority.

Everyone is entitled to look for his or her own happiness, provided that happiness does not come at a disproportionately high cost to someone else. So while of course parents are entitled to seek their own happiness with or without new partners (greater happiness for at least one person is the point of separating, after all), they are surely not entitled to allow their separation and seeking to cause their children one iota more misery than necessary. Parents (and indeed all adults) should put children ahead of themselves, not only because it's nicer for children to be happy but also because children's happiness and well-being affects the kind of people they

> **Mother of girl, aged two**
> "It goes without saying that she matters, and of course I'll see she's OK, but I don't see that she has to come first. This divorce is for me, to free me to be with someone I really love."

THE MINDFUL POLICY GROUP'S PLEDGE FOR CHILDREN

"We must put children first because we are all children first. The children we were, the children we have now, and the children they may have in the future are not our possessions or burdens: they are all of us. Children's well-being is the key to a society that is good for everyone, so ensuring it is everybody's responsibility and in everybody's interests."

Source: Mindful Policy Group 2014

will grow up to be and therefore the kind of society they will make when it's time for them to take over.

AS WELL AS each of you making your responsibilities as parents your priority, you need to agree on what those responsibilities are. They don't have to be the same for each of you. Many fathers and mothers have played very different roles in their children's lives during the marriage, and if that's how married parenting worked, divorced but mutual parenting may work similarly—or very differently. Being equally responsible as parents doesn't have to mean equality in practical arrangements for sharing the children's time and care, either; that's a different issue (see chapter 7). One way or another, though, those joint responsibilities will have to include making it possible—

> **Mother of three girls, all under five**
> "Yes, I do think separating is right for us, but I also think that we are only entitled to do it if we can protect the kids from the fallout. In fact (does this sound super-preachy?) I think we've sort of got to earn the end of our marriage by making sure of their parenting."

and enjoyable—for children to be closely in touch with each parent and, unless there is a devastatingly good reason against it, to spend time with the nonresident parent. Missing out on having a close relationship with each of you is exactly the kind of separation damage you are trying to protect them from.

If you are having trouble deciding whether you can manage mutual parenting—whether, for the children's sakes, you can each stand to be in cooperative touch rather than walk away from each other as well as from the marriage—don't rush. Give yourselves time to get over the shock of separation, and then ask yourselves whether each of you would do as much to help the other with your joint children as you would do to help your sister or your best friend with hers.

- Would you call him/expect him to call you in the middle of the night if there was an emergency, such as one child needing to be taken to the hospital and there being no one to care for the others?
- Would you discuss with him/expect him to discuss with you any worrying child behavior, such as a three-year-old going back to diapers or a nine-year-old crying easily and often?
- Would you do your best/expect him to do his best to make the transfer from one parent to the other at the beginning and end of visits easy for the children?
- Would you cover for him/expect him to cover for you if one of you had forgotten a child's sports day or school play and didn't turn up ("I expect Mommy had to work late" rather than "Just like your mom to forget")?
- Would you pay attention to each other's views on important educational decisions such as keeping a child in preschool for an extra year, choosing a school, finding the money for a school trip, or taking up a musical instrument?
- Would you pay attention to each other's views on managing children's behavior (such as how best to handle tantrums or how much fuss to make about table manners) and try to agree on routines (such as bedtimes) and limits (such as not bicycling without a helmet) so that the children met similar expectations and boundaries with each parent?

If the answer to all or most of these questions is "yes" (or "of course," "no question," or "what do you *think*?"), then you do have the foundations for mutual parenting.

A parent doesn't have to have been hands-on with the children to make parenting responsibilities a priority, although he may become more hands-on when he suddenly finds himself in full charge, and his relationships with the children will change anyway as they get older. But while mutual parenting within an intact family can work on the basis of different gender roles—accepted by both parents and by the children—mutual parenting after a separation does require at least enough blurring of those roles that each parent can operate independently of the other. Above all, it is difficult to make separated parenting mutual unless interest in the children is mutual. Giving equal head space to the children is more important than being equally hands-on. A man whose fathering has been conventional and old-fashioned may have had very little practice at changing diapers, but as long as he realizes that it matters to the toddler how diapers are changed, he can soon learn. The issue, as the points above suggest, is child-centeredness.

The mother quoted here found it difficult to imagine her children's father becoming child-centered, and it's easy to see why. But although they started from different points of view and with very different attitudes, these two *almost* managed successful mutual parenting.

> **Mother of two girls, aged five and seven, and a boy, aged nine**
>
> "Mark is a man's man. He likes women as playthings and kids for status. I've never known him to put the children ahead of his wishes; in fact, finding time to spend with them among his work and the tennis club was rare, and he always wanted me to make babysitting arrangements so we could have adults-only holidays or evenings out. He really doesn't like family treats or celebrations. In fact, I don't think he's really a family man, so how can I take him seriously when he says all the divorce business must put the kids first?"

The father, Mark, responded by saying that he felt that his main responsibility as a parent was to make generous and secure financial arrangements after the divorce. He planned to play a part in the children's lives by sharing decisions about their education and activities. He also assumed that once his ex was on her own it would be his responsibility to provide emergency backup, although he reserved the right to do that "by throwing my money at it rather than my time." Although he had never seen much of the children, he did realize that he was no longer even glimpsing them at the breakfast table, and he was looking for other ways of seeing them regularly within his own lifestyle. His most successful initiative was taking them for lessons at the tennis club each weekend, which they much enjoyed.

However, after more than a year, it gradually became clear that mutual parenting wasn't working for Mark and his ex, and the aspect that ended up being out of reach was the part that makes it work best: mother and father feeling genuinely supportive of each other in relation to the children and even retaining some respect for each other as parents. The children's mother had never respected Mark as a father, and he had little respect for the role of mother. After two or three years, they had to settle for the next best thing, which is polite parenting.

POLITE PARENTING

Some couples who understand the importance to children of their parents staying in close touch nevertheless find it impossible to achieve—or even imagine—the two-way support that is the essence of mutual parenting. Fortunately, being unable wholeheartedly to support each other doesn't mean you have to be enemies. There are lesser degrees of contact and communication that demand much less friendship but still protect the children from the worst fallout from the parental separation bomb.

Starting into polite parenting usually depends on making relatively formal arrangements, not only about dividing up money and property and about which parent the child will live with after separation but also about when and where and how the other parent will spend time with him. Since before a court will grant you a divorce or dissolve a civil partnership you have to show that you have made these arrangements, you have to discuss them (see chapter 4), and if you are both trying to be polite, you may be able to work them out between you. Often, though, parents who are struggling with civility enlist the help of lawyers to make sure that these agreements leave nothing to chance (or to unwelcome discussion).

Rigid plans backed by written documents can be only the bare bones of life after separation, though. Some couples draw up amazingly detailed documents, including lists of rules to which each signs agreement, templates for telephone calls between them, and "visit logs," which each parent must fill in before the child is transferred to the care of the other. But while drawing up such documents may make it easier for parents who can hardly bring themselves to speak to each other to talk about their children, actually using them is likely to provide one parent with a weapon to use against the other ("It says you're to bring her back by 6:30, not 6:47"), and the hope must be that they won't be needed for long. Once you have been physically apart for a few months, during which time neither of you has broken the agreements nor done anything to offend the other, the flexibility you need and the communication it takes can usually creep in. It's not unheard of for a polite parenting setup eventually to become something close to mutual.

Sometimes, though, parents have issues with each other that make even polite parenting impossible. Perhaps, for example, a father is determined to have easy access to a small child and "a fair share of her time," despite the fact that during the marriage, his fathering was of the "bedtime story when he got home early enough" kind.

Father of girl, aged three
"Come on, Maria, you've always played up what hard work it is looking after Melanie, but how hard can it be?"

If a father has never before taken sole responsibility for his child—meals and play, bath times, bedtimes and bad dreams, squabbles and safety measures—it is understandable if the mother finds it impossible to agree to any overnight visits until he has gotten to know the child. If he is determined not to settle for anything less, even for a few months, any attempts at cooperation may be stillborn.

Some fathers and mothers have always had different views on aspects of their children's upbringing. While they lived together, one parent balanced the other, and their differences didn't seem insurmountable, but once they are apart, neither parent can feel fully supportive and trusting of the other.

Being polite is even more difficult for a parent who feels that the other is (or might be) a negative influence in a child's life. For example, if one parent has always found it difficult to meet or even tolerate a child's special needs, the other parent may shudder to contemplate situations in which that parent and the child would be alone together.

These are not the kinds of

Father of two boys, aged three and four, and one girl, aged eight
"There are things to do with the kids that we just don't agree on. Like she's really anti-vaccine and into all that alternative stuff. We've often argued about it, and a few times I've actually taken one of them to the pediatrician against her wishes because I thought he needed antibiotics. What will happen when I'm not around?"

Mother of girl, aged four
"He's a good father, but he's nobody's best-ever daddy. A bit uptight. A bit cold. Very religious. He never interfered with the way I carried on with her, but she won't get much fun or much loving if I'm not there."

Mother of boy, aged six
"When Charles was a baby, his father could cope. But changing diapers on 'a big boy' and helping him feed himself with a spoon is beyond him. He says it grosses him out, and I've always done it. If the two of them were alone together, I don't think he'd leave Charles dirty or hungry, but I do think he'd make it obvious he was disgusted, and I wouldn't trust him not to try and force Charles to do things that are beyond him."

issues that both parents are likely to reach agreement on without help, but that doesn't mean they have to cause a fight. If a basic plan is arrived at, with help, perhaps, from a mediator or a lawyer, such that for the next few months at least the children will live with the father in the first example, the mother in the other two, and in each instance have daytime (rather than overnight) contact on weekends with the other parent, there is no reason why arrangements between the parents for putting the plan into action should not remain polite. If even that kind of agreement seems out of reach because both parents want to be the custodial parent or at least to have the child stay with them over weekends or holidays, or one parent wants to leave the country, taking the children with her, it is still worth attending a mediation meeting to see if you can work things out without going to court.

It is when you cannot work things out even with the help of a mediator or when the situation is more difficult still because it involves domestic violence, or physical or sexual abuse seen by or perhaps suffered by the child, that legal advice and court orders will be necessary (see pp. 91–100).

6

Trying to Get Children to Take Sides

"ALIENATION": WHAT IT MEANS AND WHY IT MATTERS

The very worst thing you can do to your children during the horrible months around your separation is to try to turn them against the other parent. You'll hear this called "alienation" by lawyers or social workers and in court. Now that we know how important it is for children to be as closely involved as possible with both parents, alienation is recognized as dreadfully damaging. In the United States and in some other parts of the world, it is actually against the law for one parent to set out to spoil a child's relationship with or feelings about the other.

When a parent sets out to alienate a child from the other parent, he or she is usually enmeshed in angry estrangement between spouses that is not being kept apart from the relationships between parents and children. Deliberate alienation uses children as weapons in an adult battle, making them even more its victims. From children's point of view, this is the most damaging, the worst way their mothers and fathers can react to separation, and it leads to the very opposite of the best: to parenting that is broken instead of mutual or even polite.

ALIENATION BY CIRCUMSTANCE OR DEFAULT

Avoiding "broken parenting" is at least as difficult as achieving "mutual parenting," and for the same reasons: adults' feelings about each other messing up their feelings for their children.

If you're a mother or father whose partner has left the family home, it's all too easy to turn your child against him or her even without meaning to. You are upset, miserable, furious—whatever your exact emotions, they are probably pretty strong—and however hard you try to conceal your feelings your child will sense them. Because you are there and the child is upset because his other parent is not, he may well take your side, turning against your soon-to-be-ex. That scenario is especially likely if, far from being part of a long process of marriage breakdown with one parent's eventual departure mutually anticipated if not exactly agreed upon, the separation was a shock to you, and you still hope, or at least wish, that the marriage can be glued together again. Children almost invariably want that, too, so that puts the two of you on the same side (and in the same house) with the other parent on the other side and somewhere else.

> **Boy, aged six, when asked "What made you so angry with your dad?," answered:**
> "Mom kept crying. She cried a lot. I hated her crying. And Dad wasn't ever there to huggle her better. And when I said to her, 'Let's go and get him,' she said, 'He just doesn't want to be here anymore.'"

If the breakup was over an affair, your child will soon realize that and may not easily forgive what he or she will probably see as a straightforward theft of one parent from the other. Children who need to blame someone find it far easier to blame an individual who isn't either parent but a cuckoo in the family nest. If the relationship that tips your marriage into separation should prove to be long lasting, establishing a good relationship between the parent's new partner and the children may be bedeviled by their continued resentment. In the meantime, the parent who has been left alone will almost always attract more of a child's (and everyone else's) sympathy, so unless you really work to prevent it (see chapter 5), the whole situation will push the children and their other parent apart.

It is miserably easy for a baby or toddler to become alienated from a parent who isn't there—let's say it's her father who has left because the statistics say that's more likely than her mother—just *because* he isn't there. Unless the two of you make a point of father and child seeing each other regularly and often from the very beginning of the separation, their relationship will loosen and eventually lapse. If one of you actually wants that to happen—perhaps because the father wants to leave the whole family behind him and make a "new life," or because you want to punish him, or perhaps because neither of you wants anything whatsoever to do with the other—all you have to do is keep them mostly apart for several months. A shockingly large number of confused, angry women do just that, perhaps not realizing that their beloved child who has done nothing wrong suffers at least as much as her dad.

If a baby, under a year old, doesn't spend any time with her father for weeks or months, the attachment between them that should have been building toward a peak in the second year doesn't grow. She will not "forget" him. Whatever relationship she had with her father while he lived in the same home played a part in the way her brain and nervous system developed in her first months (see pp. 21–37), so he is forever part of who she is. But the area of her brain that stores memories is not yet developed enough for her consciously to remember him for long. If he is out of sight for months, he will also be out of her conscious mind. She will not be aware of missing him because the space in her life that he used to occupy will close up.

It's different if a child is two or three years old when the breakup happens. If he has made a close bond with the father during his short life before the separation, he will be very aware of his father's departure and absence and in the beginning will probably badly miss specific things they used to do together. But over a few months he will get used to his father not being there and will adapt to the new lifestyle. If a reconciliation brought Daddy home, he would probably still be delighted, but suddenly being expected to leave Mom and home and go out with him (perhaps because the father has just been granted legal access) is a different matter. Daddy doesn't mean anything clear-cut to him. In fact, he may not really understand who this man is. He may be shy and reluctant. A toddler's very natural tendency to hang back—probably with both arms firmly around his mother's thigh—is a potent weapon in an undeclared alienation war. His father, who was looking forward to excited greetings and hugs from his child, will feel devastatingly sad and rejected, especially if he has been fighting hard for the right to spend time with him. His mother will probably feel vindicated, or at least excused for her part in keeping them apart. Clearly the child does not want to be with the father, and surely he should not be forced? By the time that question gets back to conciliation or court, another few weeks, even months, will have passed and that child, now three years old, has little remaining conscious memory of this man.

> **Grandmother of girl, aged three**
>
> "Mary's not four yet. She can't get her arms around the mailbox that stands outside her front door, but it's a sturdy, familiar landmark, and she's going to hang on to it whatever all the grown-ups say about Daddy taking her for a treat. I think she knows she's being conned. Treats have Mommy in them. Or me. Or maybe Lucy's mom (she's good at treats)."

Yet another year or two on, at four or five, that shyness with and reluctance to go with a scarcely known visiting father may take on a desperate intensity, with the child tearful and panicky when the father comes to pick her up. The extreme reaction is usually not to being with the father but to being taken away from the mother. Look at it from the child's point of view: Daddy left, so how can she be sure that if she takes her eyes off Mommy, she won't leave, too (see chapter 8)?

A scene like that is agony for everybody. For the child, who is submerged in the worst kind of fear there is for a child that age:

fear of losing her main attachment figure. For the mother, who hates to see her so upset (and hates the father for making her that way), and of course for the father, who is being made to feel like an insensitive brute for wanting to spend time with the daughter he loves. Probably nobody meant father and child to become alienated, but they have.

If a child's relationship with his or her father is protected and facilitated from the beginning, even though the two of them don't live in the same house anymore (see chapter 5), painful separation scenes like this can usually be avoided. But not always. Separation anxiety is ordinary in one- to three-year-olds and by no means unusual for another two or three years, especially when family stresses make children feel insecure (see chapter 8). But if it is not unusual for "contact arrangements" to blow up, it is vital not to abandon contact altogether. For babies, toddlers, and preschool children there is one particular solution that's guaranteed from the child's point of view, though it can be tough on parents: let her father come to the child's home to spend time with her and, if necessary, have Mom hanging around in the background so she feels safe.

Understandable though Mary's mother's feelings are, they belong to her own adult relationship as woman-to-man, not to Mary's relationship with her father. Some agreed-upon grown-up ground rules might help in situations like these. For example, you might agree that child and father stay downstairs or in the bit of the home where she normally plays; that he uses the downstairs bathroom and doesn't go upstairs; and that he only gets cups of coffee if you offer.

> **Mary's mother**
> "I couldn't have him in the house, playing with Mary as if he was still family, seeing my things, drinking my coffee as if he lived there . . ."

If you really cannot bring yourself to let your ex spend time in the home even though you can see that it's the best way for your small child to spend happy time with him, a compromise may work. If there is a grandparent, aunt, or friend the child feels close to and whose house she often visits, meeting her father there may enable her to enjoy being with him. Meeting at her grandmother's house worked for Mary, and when her grandmother went away on vacation, Mary and her father were made welcome by Lucy's mom.

"Enjoy" is the key point, of course. If going out with Dad floods a child with anxiety and she is more or less forced to go, she will get minimal pleasure from this visit and, remembering her own anxious feelings, may dread the next. On the other hand, the more she enjoys whatever time she spends with her father and looks forward to seeing him again, the more self-sustaining their relationship will be.

Using Your Child as a Go-Between

If you are not seeing your ex but your child is, it's very convenient to use your child as a messenger and very tempting to extract information from her. Don't. Even if you and your ex are on "polite" terms, the messages you send are entirely practical, and the questions you ask are completely casual (*How was Daddy today? Was he cheerful?*), being used as a go-between mixes the child into the failed marital relationship when she ought to be allowed to think only about the successful parental one. If she wants to tell you what she's been doing, that's great (*How was your day?*), but don't ask her about her father. She'll volunteer anything she wants you to know.

When you need to communicate with your ex, just do it. That was far more difficult a generation ago than it is now. Thanks to cell phones, you don't have to be in a specific place at a particular time of day to receive a call or worry that if you call your ex's new girlfriend or boss might answer. If you want to make contact but you don't want to have to speak to your ex, you can send a text or an e-mail. If there are things you need to show— documents, items in catalogues you're hoping the children can have for Christmas—using a video-call service such as Skype can save you the time and emotional effort of meeting face-to-face, and save you money, too. However you choose to do it, your children's day-to-day well-being depends on the two of you being willing and able to communicate and to keep your communication between the two of you.

The less friendly, or even polite, the terms you are on, the worse it is for your child to play go-between, because every message risks conveying subtle criticism. The child will pick up on that and feel that he's being forced to share it.

"Tell your dad not to forget it's your concert next Saturday" sounds harmless but isn't: it clearly suggests to the child that his father is likely to forget an event that's important to him. Almost all "reminders" also subtly convey the superiority of the parent who sends them over the recipient. "I know when sports day or spring break is because I'm the parent in the know; he won't know unless I tell him and won't remember unless I remind him."

> **Boy, aged fourteen**
> "My mom really tried not to be nosy, not even to ask questions when I'd been out with Dad. But the atmosphere kind of stank of unasked questions, and it got worse as I got older. One day—it must have been about a year ago, so I'd have been thirteen—we went out together, and when I got home, Mom asked if I'd had a nice time, and that was OK: I said yes, it had been fine. But then she asked me how my dad was, and I managed to say he was fine, too. But then she tried one more question (the one she'd been building up to all along, as if I didn't realize that), how did his new job seem to be going? And I just blew up and told her, 'If you really want to know, ask him yourself.'"

Even people who are not friends can e-mail, so the "if you have something to say to each other, do it directly" rule still holds (but take care to read through your message before you press "send"). Remember, though, that when it comes to keeping track of day care or school dates and events, each of you has an equal right to be kept informed by the school. If the school still communicates via those pieces of paper that end up crumpled in the bottom of your child's bag, a copy should routinely go in the mail to the nonresident parent. If it isn't happening, it's because nobody has told the school that the child's two parents live apart. Do it. If the school uses e-mail or expects parents to check its website, make sure the office has both e-mail addresses.

ANGRY ALIENATION AND ITS USE AS A WEAPON IN ADULT CONFLICT

A parent who lets a child get involved in the adult war that's raging in and around the household or even deliberately uses her as a weapon against the other parent probably doesn't mean their child any harm. She may be one of many women who feel that, unlike being a mother, being a father is an earned privilege that men can lose through bad behavior, and who don't think about the spin-off effects on the children. Or he may be so full of fury at the woman who has betrayed him that he thinks he's actually right to protect the child from her mother.

However well-meaning such a parent's motives, and whatever the individual circumstances, deliberate alienation is wrong, and the lengths to which some alienating parents will go and the damage they cause to their children are truly shocking.

When a father has left the family home, some mothers will lie and cheat to keep him and their child from speaking to or seeing each other and to lessen the father in the child's eyes:

TO FATHER: He can't come to the phone; he's in the bath.
TO CHILD: No, it was not your father. Do you really think he's going to bother calling?

TO FATHER: She told me to tell you she doesn't want to speak to you.
TO CHILD: Yes, it was him. Drunk as usual. I told him he wasn't fit to speak to you.

TO FATHER ON DOORSTEP: They're not coming out with you; they've gone to their grammy's.

TO CHILDREN: You didn't want to go with him and leave me all
   by myself, did you?

Examples such as these may sound trivial, but cumulatively they
are toxic.

Some parents, men as well as women, will share their own
hateful feelings with children, encouraging them not only to see
the absent one in a bad light now but also to lose faith in the family relationships they used to take for granted:

> She's never been any good; I never would have married her,
> but then I found out she was expecting. She's not much of a
> mother. Yes, of course you thought you loved her, but that's
> where she's sneaky. She turns on the charm, and people
> believe it.

Perhaps cruelest of all, some parents solicit sympathy from
children who love them, making it seem disloyal of them to love
the other parent:

> Don't you leave me, too . . . You're all I've got. Every time I
> see you hug him it's like someone stabbed me . . . We're all
> right together, aren't we? We don't need him.

Nonresident parents are in a weak position compared with
the parents that children live with. A lot of them are sufficiently
intimidated by this kind of behavior that the alienation actually
works; the relationships between parents and children shrivel
and visits gradually stop.

When a nonresident parent will not be put off but is insistent
on seeing the children, and especially if both parents have been
through mediation or the nonresident parent seeks advice from a
lawyer, the resident parent may become aware that she cannot
continue refusing to let the children see their father without a
very good reason, and a few will set about producing one. She
may go to a social worker or lawyer saying that there has been

sexual abuse or domestic violence. Or that there is some other reason to think that the child might be at risk; that the nonresident parent's environment would be unsafe or a bad influence (alcoholism, drug addiction, and mental illness may be mentioned) or that, given the opportunity, the other parent will take the child away, possibly out of the country.

Such claims may or may not be accurate, but because they are about child protection (the court's principal concern), they will have to be investigated before visitation is resumed. Even if the children are not old enough to understand what their mother is saying about their father, just putting forward such accusations almost always has an alienating effect. Even if the accusations are without foundation and totally denied by the father, who sees them as part of a deliberate attempt to alienate the children from him, they have to be investigated. In the meantime, once he has been accused, he cannot continue to insist on seeing the children—and certainly must not attempt to do so without the mother's knowledge or against her wishes. Instead, he will have to apply to the court for a contact order (see pp. 91–100). The date for hearing such an order may be set months ahead, which could mean that the child does not see

> **Father of girl, now aged eight, and boy, now aged six**
>
> "At the time I just couldn't stand it. Going down every Saturday—three buses and almost sixty bucks—and then finding that the kids weren't there—or she said they weren't—or they were there, but she made such a performance about where I was taking them that she really made it sound like I was going to kidnap them. Once they were crying and saying they didn't want to come with me, she'd get all reasonable and say, 'It's only Daddy. I'm sure he'll take you on a nice walk,' but it was too late then. The last time she actually said 'I'm so sorry, Marty' (all superior). 'I'm doing my best, but it's not my fault they don't love you anymore.' She's lucky I didn't slap her.
>
> "I wish now I'd gone on somehow. Maybe I should have gone back to the lawyer. But that already bankrupted me once, and anyway I was—how to put it?—offended. These are my kids, and she shamed me with them, and now it's almost two years since I saw them and it's too late."

him at all during that period and as a result their relationship is further damaged.

Sometimes the claims a resident parent makes against the other parent strike him as outrageous. If they are produced out of the blue, having never been mentioned during preceding months of legal wrangling, it may be difficult for him to understand why anyone takes any notice. However, if there is the least chance that the father has been abusive, he cannot be allowed unsupervised contact with the child until the matter has been investigated. On the other hand, the court recognizes the importance to children of contact with both parents and must try to balance the two. Supervised contact, at a contact center or at the home of an approved relative, is the court's best available compromise. However insulting it may feel to the parent and however inadequate to the children's needs, it is better than no contact at all, and it is usually assumed to be temporary. If all goes well, the nonresident parent can apply after a few months to have contact liberalized.

SOMETIMES ONE PARENT'S EFFORTS to alienate children from the other parent are more than a reaction to immediate anger or hurt and a desire to protect the children but are intentionally harmful: weapons wielded by a vengeful ex-partner in an ongoing adult war and intended not only to reduce children's contact with the absent parent but also to damage him or her in every aspect of adult life. In the example below there had been escalating quarrels within the marriage, and when it disintegrated, both mother and father sought to be the resident parent, each claiming that the other was unfit:

> Michael alleged that Lizbeth was a problem drinker and that it was when she was drunk that their fights escalated. Lizbeth denied getting drunk although she did admit to heavier drinking due to the stress of marriage problems and Michael's anger.
>
> Lizbeth alleged that Michael pushed her on several occa-

sions and maintained that the children saw the fighting on at least one occasion. She further alleged that Michael once threw a frying pan at her, after which she called the police. It was this incident that led to the separation and to Lizbeth going to court to ask for residence and contact orders.

Michael denied the domestic violence. He maintained that far from throwing the frying pan at Lizbeth, he was trying to restrain her and in doing so the pan was knocked off the stove.

Since the separation, the children have lived with their mother and been allowed only daytime visits with their father. When he applied to the court to amend contact, Lizbeth stated that the children were traumatized by the incident involving the frying pan and the police and were frightened of Michael's anger.

In addition, warned by her attorney that she did not have the sympathy of the judge, Lizbeth put in a new statement telling the court that she is concerned that Michael cannot be trusted to maintain appropriate sexual boundaries with the children.

Michael alleges that Lizbeth is attempting to alienate the children from him by exaggerating the violence and denying her contribution to it, and now by planning to accuse him of sexual abuse of the children.

Whether the final step in the escalating accusations was factually true or not, that angry couple had trapped their children in a double bind of damage. If a child is sexually abused by a parent, the psychological damage can last a lifetime. But if a child who has not been abused is falsely led to believe that a loving parent harmed him or her, that distortion of reality can itself cause long-lasting psychological harm.

This is why allegations of parent incest trump all other weapons in alienation wars. When a parent makes that accusation to a mediator, social worker, lawyer, or in court, it is clear that the child needs protection, but it is not clear if the immediate need is for protection from the alleged offender or protection from false information by the accusing parent. The court must investigate the allegations and decide if they are true or not, but until all the evidence is weighed, a balance ought to be struck that does not favor one parent over another. Because priority is usually given to protecting the child from abuse, courts often order that the child have no contact with the allegedly abusive parent until a comprehensive evaluation of the family dynamics has been made by experts and utilized by the court to make a determination.

Mother of two girls, aged six and nine
"It wasn't really my fault. I didn't say he had, I only said he might. Anyway, I didn't actually mean it. I just didn't want him taking my girls away from me every weekend. Somehow it got around, though, and the children were interviewed and the school knew, and then I absolutely tried to stop it but I couldn't. In the end Eric was pushed out of his job—he was manager of a local supermarket—and his new woman walked out on him, and he can't pay what he's meant to in maintenance."

Whatever the truth of the original accusation or the eventual outcome of proceedings, sexual abuse allegations ruin lives. Not only the lives of men (and occasionally women) whose ex-partners have accused them of abusing their mutual children but also the lives of the children whose relationships with the accused parent will never recover. An allegation of sexual abuse can be dismissed as groundless, found unproven, even withdrawn, but it cannot be unmade. Men, even some whose ex-wives never really believed their own accusations but made them so as to keep access to a minimum, have lost jobs and friends as well as their children.

AVOIDING ALIENATION WHEN AGREEMENT SEEMS IMPOSSIBLE

If you are really convinced that it is important to your children to have the best possible relationship with both parents and you are therefore really determined to avoid alienating them from the

PROTECTING CHILDREN'S ATTACHMENTS WHILE ALLEGATIONS AGAINST PARENTS ARE INVESTIGATED

In California and Florida, attorneys and the courts have crafted plans so that when an accusation of sexual abuse is made by a parent, the identified child continues to have a relationship with both parents while being protected from harm caused by either of them. The success of these unique plans rests on the ability of the legal professionals to find an agreeable alternative living situation that will not be traumatic for the child as the investigation proceeds. One such plan involves a neutral adult (such as a friend of the family or family member) known to have a positive relationship with the child who is awarded temporary legal care of the child. The designated adult may move into the family home and the parents temporarily move into another residence, or the child may move into the temporary caretaker's home. Frequent contact (often daily) with the child is awarded to the mother and father and may be supervised by the child's temporary legal guardian.

Another proposed plan involves a neutral family friend or member temporarily relocating to the state of legal jurisdiction for the divorce and then renting an apartment in which he or she will live with the child. Temporary guardianship is awarded to this adult, who may act in the role of supervisor when the child has frequent scheduled visits with his or her parents.

These unique arrangements allow the child to maintain attachment relationships with both the mother and father while being protected both from potential sexual abuse by one parent and from destruction of a healthy attachment by the false accusations of the other. Although critics might question the appropriateness of the child being temporarily separated from both parents, a commonplace alternative (and the usual measure in the United Kingdom) is removal of the child into foster care with strangers. The California and Florida arrangements are certainly a less traumatizing way of accomplishing the essential protection of the child from potential sexual and psychological abuse and altered memories, as well as providing sufficient time for a careful and thorough investigation.

other parent—let's say the mother—you can do it, even if there is no room for agreement or even politeness between you. There are arrangements that will ensure that your child can have contact with her without risk, and there are people and organizations who can help you to make them.

When One Parent Thinks the Other Is Unfit

If you genuinely believe that your ex-partner is unfit to take sole charge of the children, you will obviously try to make sure that doesn't happen. Making allegations of abuse, addiction, or dangerous neglect may seem the easiest way, but quite apart from their immorality, inaccurate or wildly exaggerated accusations may damage rather than protect the children. If you avoid alienating the children from her, even a mother who cannot take care of them on her own may still be able to have a loving relationship with them, and while their safety and well-being is of course your first priority, the best possible relationship with the other parent comes close behind.

How easy or difficult it is to make arrangements that meet both those demands mostly depends on your own relationship with your ex. If she recognizes her own shortcomings as a parent in sole charge, is as anxious as you are about the children's safety, and is grateful to you for encouraging her contact with them, you may be able

Father of boy, aged seven, and girl, aged five
"At the moment she's in rehab. She's an addict to just about any mind-altering stuff you can think of. She seems to get hooked on whatever's available, and some of the mixtures she's taken in the last couple of years have been really dangerous. Last time I was away for work, there was a fire. She didn't even wake up, but the kids got her out. They were six and four then. That was the last straw. I couldn't pretend that she could be in charge of them anymore. Luckily, she knows. She loves them and she knows she can't be sure to keep them safe, so she hasn't fought me. The kids see her during visiting hours, and when she comes out, she'll probably come and see them here or in the summer they could go to the park with friends. She can't mother them, but she's still their mother."

to make arrangements between you. That may sound like a very big "if," but it does sometimes happen.

Of course, most parents are not so accepting of being judged "unfit," and many are extremely reluctant to abide by any restrictions that their ex-partners try to impose on their contact with the children, especially if there is no objective evidence against them, such as a relevant medical condition, criminal record, police warning, or referral to social services. The most frequent focus for anxiety is overnight visits (see pp. 152–70), and it is these that many parents—like the two quoted in this section—seek to prevent. Sometimes the resident parent's long and intimate knowledge of the other parent is enough to worry him or her. For instance, if a father has been irritable and not at all child-centered during the marriage, the mother may know that he will have no idea how to cope with the child's evening and bedtime routine and that he might lose his temper with the child if things went wrong. Sometimes, though, a father simply finds the prospect of the child being out of his care overnight intolerable, so

> **Mother of two girls, aged eight and six**
> "I divorced him when they were only three and one, so I guess I could have sort of dropped him out of their lives. He was an alcoholic, and family life just wasn't possible, but he was—and is—a nice man and he loved them and still does, so I didn't want to take all that away. He sees them every week and always has. I wouldn't let them go away and stay with him, because he might not be responsible, but he knows that himself and wouldn't ask. But they're perfectly safe going out with him in the daytime. They're movie buffs, all three of them."

every aspect of the mother's potential care strikes him as unacceptable. He may raise the specter of neglect over trivial matters, such as the mother's habit of watching TV with the volume so high that he fears she might not hear the child if he woke, as well as over truly dangerous possibilities such as leaving the sleeping child alone in the house.

If you are generally managing polite if not mutual parenting, you may be able to talk through and resolve anxieties and arrive at mutually acceptable living arrangements for the children and visiting plans for the nonresident parent. However, you may find yourselves caught up in a vicious circle where a parent's anger and humiliation at not being trusted with his or her own child builds up to a point where agreed arrangements are broken and the ex-partner's suspicions about untrustworthiness are confirmed. The breaches may be trivial—bringing the child back a few minutes late, perhaps, or buying him a disapproved snack—but sometimes they are more serious.

> We agreed that he could take her to spend Saturday with his mother. The second time he did it he called me to say they'd missed the train and would have to stay over. It was just an excuse. He did it on purpose. I just can't trust him to stick to what we've worked out.

If it proves impossible for both of you to honor shared arrangements, you may need the help of the court in imposing them.

When One Parent Has Been Shown to Be Unfit

If your ex was physically abusive to one of the children, or to you—perhaps in sight of the children—or has been shown to have sexually abused one of the children, or if he has been convicted of some other appalling crime, then it's entirely understandable if you do not want him to have anything further to do with you or the children. But even if your desire to airbrush him right out of all your lives and what is left of your family is almost overwhelming, it is not ultimately desirable from your children's point of view. Hopefully, when your shock, fury, and disgust at his behavior begin to let up, you will see that you can't and shouldn't deny his existence or his identity altogether and that the law won't help you.

First the "can't." Whatever this man has done, he exists, and however much you wish it weren't so, he is your children's biological father. To wipe him out, you'd have to be prepared to tell whopping lies to the children when eventually they ask about their dad and to your family and friends and neighbors, too. If he left and you remarried when the children were tiny, you might pretend that your second husband, their stepfather, is their father. If the children were old enough when he left to remember their father, you might tell them he is dead. But quite apart from the rights and wrongs of lying, you would certainly get caught out eventually, and that would be the end of trust in your family.

Now the "shouldn't." All children have a deep-seated need to know about their parents and where they came from. You only have to look on the Internet to see that huge numbers of people spend hours trying to trace their lost beginnings. Most people accept that need in adopted or foster children, and nowadays we take trouble to be open with them so that they can ask questions when they're ready and deal with truthful answers even if they're painful. That need is exactly the same for children like yours whose fathers are absent because they abused them or you or are in prison for other awful crimes.

Mothers shouldn't try to airbrush even abusive fathers out of children's lives, but that does not mean that they should invite those fathers in. If you are genuinely afraid of your ex, you have every right to refuse to see him, and the court system will support you. But if he goes to court asking to be allowed contact with the children, the court will not automatically refuse it because of what he did in the past, because being a father is not conditional on good behavior, and children have a right to the best possible relationship with both parents.

The court will call experts to explore the father's motives for seeking contact (does he really love the children or is he trying to use them to keep power over you?). Those experts will seek to understand what happened in your ex's childhood that contributed to his crimes, and to assess the dynamics of the family. A good court assessment can go a long way to explaining what might have gone wrong in the parental relationship and to helping work out if it will be safe for the children to see their father or have any contact with him. Those assessments will also help to establish how the children really feel about their dad. Research shows that children are often so desperate not to hurt the parent they live with that they will say what they know she wants to hear rather what they actually feel. That can mean that yours say bad things about their father and say they don't want any contact with him when truthfully, like it or not, they love him.

After an expert assessment, the court will decide whether your ex should be allowed to have contact with the children, and if so, what kind and how much. You might find yourself ordered to allow him to see them regularly on his own; to have regular supervised visits with them in an approved place, such as a grandparent's home; not to see them but to talk to them on the phone or text, e-mail, or write to them; or to have no direct contact with them but to send letters, birthday cards, and perhaps presents via a lawyer.

The judgment the court makes may not be one that either you or your ex would have chosen, allowing him less contact than he asked for but more than you want him to have. However, if a full assessment has been carried out, the expert report on which the court's decision is based will probably get it right for the children, and that is what matters most.

7

Sharing Parenting

When spouses separate, they stop being a couple, but they don't stop being parents. Irrespective of who left whom or why, neither father nor mother is any less a parent than before the breakup. It took two of you to make your babies, and neither of you could ever stop being their parent even if you wanted to. The importance to children of contact with both their parents during and after family breakdown cannot be overstated, and in the last ten years has been increasingly widely recognized in family law. Indeed, legal recognition of parents' equality is mandatory in the United States, Australia, and the United Kingdom. But if it is now generally accepted that separated mothers and fathers are equally parents, it is not generally agreed what being a parent means: the role that follows the fact. If you are equally parents, does that automatically mean that your parenting is equal, and if so, is that equality a matter of quality, quantity, or both? In Australia, when legal recognition of the equality of separating parents first became mandatory, it was widely interpreted to mean both: fathers were to be viewed and dealt with in the courts as equally important as mothers and to have equal rights of access to the children. In the United States—and now in the United Kingdom—the emphasis is on quality rather than quantity and on children's rather than parents' rights. Fathers' equal importance is more a matter of being equally as concerned for the children as the mother and equally responsible for ensuring their well-being than a matter of spending equal time with them.

A COUPLE APPLYING for a divorce must say which parent the children are to live with: the "custodial parent," or, where there is joint custody, the "resident parent" or "parent with care"; how access for the nonresident or "contact parent" will be arranged, and who will pay what for the children's maintenance (see pp. 86–100). It is usually accepted that most children will live more with one parent than the other (school makes that almost inevitable for over-fives) and that the parent the child mostly lives with will be the resident parent. She will be the one who can claim any child-related tax benefits and to whom child support must be paid.

But those answers to the court's questions are largely legal formalities. The practicalities of sharing parenting may be a different matter, because as long as separating parents are in agreement with each other and submit a joint, uncontested plan, they can make whatever actual arrangements they please. Nobody else cares whether the children really are spending more time with the resident parent than the other, and of course there is nothing to stop parents from sharing benefits or arranging support between them. So the two of you have the freedom and the responsibility to answer these crucial questions: Where and with whom are your children going to live? When and how is the other parent to see them? The questions are easier to ask than to answer. Arranging what you will hear lawyers or social workers call "contact" or "access" for the parent whom the children don't actually live with is both one of the most important and one of the most difficult parts of post-separation life.

TOWARD CHILD-CENTEREDNESS

From King Solomon–like Solutions to Child-Centered Parenting Plans

Everyone surely has to accept that mothers and fathers are equally *parents;* it is a biological fact, after all. But equal or shared *parenting* is a different matter that is widely misunderstood to mean that a mother and father ought to have as near half shares of their children as is practically possible. Sometimes half shares mean literally half of the children, cutting a family of siblings in two with one or more children going with Mom and another with Dad. More often it means half of each child, cutting his or her time down the middle so that roughly half the time is spent with one parent and half with the other. None of that is quite as horrible as King Solomon's suggestion that the baby over whom two women were quarreling should be cut in two so they could each have half, but whereas his suggestion was impossible (which is why it brought the women to their senses), these modern versions unfortunately are not, and once they are in place they often have their own inertia, so that parents don't feel the need to think again. Consider carefully before you embark on trying to make a fair division of your children, or of one child's time and presence, between the two of you. If you stand back a little, you will see that if you do this you are treating your children as if they are commodities, marital property to be shared like the furniture or the money in that joint account. Such an approach to sharing parenting is never the best and is often the worst option, seriously damaging to children whose lives are salami-sliced.

All over the Western world there are babies, toddlers, schoolchildren, and adolescents who are uprooted at more or less regular and frequent intervals from one parent's home and moved to the other's; they may never be sure which is actually home for them. There are parenting plans that require children to spend Sunday night to Wednesday afternoon in one household,

Wednesday night to Sunday afternoon in the other. Some children spend alternate whole weeks with each parent and some alternate school terms. Probably the most common arrangement is for children to spend weekdays with one parent and weekends or alternate weekends with the other. This last arrangement is popular with adults because, if the weekend covers Friday afternoon to Monday morning, it gives parents almost "fair shares" of the children, and that division often fits with children's school schedules and the nonresident parent's working hours. It may or may not be popular with children. In some (usually well-to-do) communities, living and working in one place (usually thought of as home) and retreating to another place for weekends is not unusual. If it makes a life pattern that a child settles into and eventually enjoys, this plan may work well for everyone. Don't take it for granted, though. As with every other aspect of coping with family breakdown, you need to consider your own individual children.

Even when routine week-by-week arrangements are comfortable for children as well as adults, King Solomon often reappears on holidays. Many children must eat two

Boy, aged ten

"All my school sports things are on Saturday, and now that I'm ten I'm on the teams. Soccer now; tennis in the summer. When they started talking about me going to my dad's on weekends, I did try to remind them about that, but they didn't really take much notice. Dad said he'd drive me to school on Saturdays, but we only did it once 'cause he said it was too far. I asked Mom if I could just go to Dad's on Saturday afternoon after the games are over, but she said that wouldn't be fair, as Dad would only have me for one night. I think this way is not very fair to me."

Girl, aged twelve

"Mom gets all the homework hassles and washing school clothes and driving to after-school stuff. We don't ever get to see each other in the daytime 'cause I'm at school, and we don't get to go out or have much fun time together in the evenings because it's always school again the next day. Sometimes I wish I could be with my dad when it's math homework and be with my mom for a Saturday's shopping."

Mother on half-week custody arrangement:
"It works for me because I know exactly when he'll be with me and when I can have time off from mothering without having to pay a babysitter."

Her ex
"It's OK. He comes. His days are in my calendar for the rest of the school year. His mother and I don't have to meet or discuss it. It's not perfect though, a bit rigid already, and that'll get worse when he's older. Already it's tricky keeping to it during vacations when he wants to have particular kids over and he's in the wrong place. It would work better if we lived even closer together. Special celebrations are tricky, too. Does he just spend his birthday with whichever parent he happens to be with on the day it falls? And Christmas—well, we've already had one of those and it was miserable."

Their son, aged eight
"I'd just like to live somewhere and visit the other place. Other kids go home; I go to my dad's or to my mom's."

Christmas dinners, often one on the day and the other a day or so sooner or later, and can only have school friends to their birthday parties every other year because on the alternate years it's the other parent's turn and the birthday celebration is too far away for school friends to join in. Dividing up these special days is very difficult ("heartbreaking" might be a better word) and very individual, but it matters to children and can be done better. There are some suggestions from parents in chapter 9.

A King Solomon approach to sharing parenting works for many mothers and fathers, and because they tend to be overwhelmed with the adult aspects of their separation, most of them do not even take the time to wonder if it's the best possible arrangement for their child or children. The nonresident parent—nine times out of ten, the father—often wants his fair share of the children at almost any cost. He may feel, and advisers from his own mother to his attorney may tell him, that it's his right. Some fathers involved in arguments over arrangements for the children even feel that settling for less than the nearest possible to a fifty-fifty division of their time and presence might make his ex or the children themselves feel that he didn't care about them. The resident—and now single—parent, the mother in this example, would often prefer the children to live with her full-time but usually acknowledges—or is forced by her lawyer to acknowledge—the justice of their father's case. Sometimes, though, a mother may be far from reluctant for the children to spend time with their father. She may feel that it is only fair to her that her ex shares the child care burden, giving her predictable stretches of child-free time and the opportunity to get a new life going.

Wanting more, and less, of children's presence and direct responsibility for their care is understandable, but scenarios like these can never be acceptable because they do not accommodate children's feelings and choices. A child needs to meet family breakdown as his own person rather than as his parents' treat or burden.

Each of your children's lives belongs to him or her, not to either or both of you. It is the breakup of your marriage or other adult partnership that has made it necessary to formalize parenting into something shared between the two of you individuals rather than enjoyed by you both as a couple, and in this situation it is children's rights that are in question rather than yours. It is every child's right to maintain the best possible relationship with each parent, and it is your joint responsibility to facilitate that as best you can. As equal parents you each have one and only one right to a child: the right to opportunities to maintain a loving, caring relationship with her. That means, of course, that neither of you is entitled to try to belittle the other parent in your child's eyes (see chapter 6), or to sabotage their communication, or to prevent them from seeing each other unless there is evidence that contact is unsafe.

PARENTING PLANS

Parents, children, and parenting plans are individual, so no outsider—or even paid adviser—can tell you exactly what you should arrange. However, in the light of recent research, there are some basic recommendations and pitfalls that really do seem to apply to parents and children in general: parents in civil partnerships or same-sex marriages as well as heterosexual married couples, and adopted as well as biological children from infants to adults. Most of them have been discussed in detail in earlier chapters, but the ones that are most important to your immediate decision making are summarized here.

- Children's current and future happiness and well-being should be central to whatever parenting plans you make. Understandably, a parent sometimes demands to know why: "Why should children have priority? What about my happiness? Doesn't that matter just as much?" Of course the happiness of both parents matters—indeed, it is probably a search for some kind of happiness for at least one of you that led to the breakdown of your family—but where your happiness and your children's happiness are at odds, theirs must come first, because while you are already formed adults, their lifelong development and their adult personalities, achievements, and relationships depend on their emotional well-being throughout childhood. Having their family disintegrate and their parents living apart will in itself make children anxious and unhappy, which is why it's not something any loving parent undertakes lightly. But by understanding which aspects of the new situation are most upsetting for this particular child at this particular time, and by working to avoid or modify those even if you have to do so at your own expense, you can do a great deal to soften the impact (see chapters 2 and 4).
- For many children, the most important aspect of their parents' separation is not the obvious one—a parent moving out of the home to live elsewhere—but their mother's and father's ongoing relationship, or lack of it. In fact, most children are more upset by the hateful atmosphere and endless arguments (or worse) that surround family breakdown than they are by

the separation itself. The least traumatic parental separation for children is one in which the mother and father can remain respectful of each other as joint parents even though they reject each other as partners (see chapter 5). The most destructive separation is one where the couple's relationship becomes so toxic that one or both parents try to put the children off the other one and to persuade them to take sides (see chapter 6).

- Even if neither parent deliberately tries to alienate the children from the other, either or both may be so overwhelmed with anger, jealousy, guilt, and self-loathing that even when they are physically with their children, they are emotionally absent. That kind of absence is as damaging as the physical kind. Preserving space for children in heads and hearts, desperately difficult though it may sometimes be, is the bedrock of their continued well-being, which is why "mutual parenting" (see pp. 108–13) is the ideal to strive for. If both parents can manage to keep that space for their children, emotionally and practically, they may grow up unscathed (though not unchanged) by the separation.

- However mutual the parenting you are struggling toward, there will certainly be upsets, especially at the beginning of life apart. When you are trying to get your toddler to bed and he's mixing hitting out at you with clinging to you, it's desperately depressing to realize that he's missing Daddy's bedtime routine and stories and that yours aren't a satisfactory substitute. And when it's Friday night and you've made the especially nice dinner that tradition demands, but the older children turn sulky and unhelpful, it's demoralizing to realize that a special Friday night dinner was a family tradition and they're missing the family part although you've provided the traditional meal. There will probably be many times like these when, however hard you are both trying to be supportive of each other as parents, it's impossible not to be angry and/or feel guilty on your children's behalf.

You can see that they are suffering from the breakdown of their family and you know that the two of you brought it upon them. In the long term, though, rage and remorse for what's past won't help as much as thinking positively about the future. When the current storms die down, your separation need not prevent your children from being happy. Many children in so-called intact families grow up and flourish while one parent works away from home for substantial periods of time. There are even some children whose securely married parents choose to occupy separate homes and visit each other. If there is a single overwhelming difference between those children and yours, it is that their parents are united though apart, and their children know it. You two are not united (and your children know it), but mutual parenting can come to mean that you are at one where they are concerned: that you parent together although you're apart.

■ Assessing and understanding children's happiness and well-being is crucial and must depend on their ages and stages of development and on careful observation of their behavior (see chapter 2). A teenager can and should be consulted about all plans that involve him, and he may often be allowed to choose. A baby cannot choose, and her contentment with arrangements can be judged only by concentrated attention to her behavior and not being too ready to ascribe everything undesirable to teething. Between those extremes, a three-year-old's distress at the prospect of spending a weekend away from her mom or a six-year-old's sudden anxiety about going to school should certainly be heard and carefully thought about but should not always be directly acted upon, because immediate happiness and long-term well-being may not be the same (see chapter 1). Often, though, immediate happiness and long-term well-being *are* the same, and if your eight- or eleven-year-old feels able to talk to you and sure that you will hear, he may tell you what he is missing most; she may tell you what keeps making her cry, and you may be able to put a Band-Aid on the worst wounds.

■ Parenting plans need to be regular and predictable enough that all concerned—adults as well as children—can rely on them and come to take them for granted instead of wasting time and energy planning (and arguing) week by week. If it is part of the agreement that you will drive the children to meet up with their father each Sunday (perhaps because the family car has stayed with you), doing so must be a real commitment; and if their father is due to visit at a particular time on a particular day, he must be there more or less on the dot, always.

■ But within the regularity that will help children come to feel safe and secure in the new arrangements, there also needs to be some flexibility, both week by week and in the long term, and this is yet another instance of mutual parenting scoring more highly than any alternative type. The fact that the father routinely brings the toddler home to his mother at 7 p.m. on Sunday evenings should not mean that he cannot be brought home an hour earlier on one particular Sunday when his grandparents are to visit his mother at 6 p.m. Only a desire to assert himself over the mother could make a father refuse to sacrifice that single hour to a visit that will be a treat for the child (and the grandparents). On another Sunday you may find yourself grumbling that 7 p.m. is not 7:10—it isn't, of course, but the traffic may think that it is. Niggling insistence from either of you on the other parent sticking to the very letter of your arrangements will suggest that your parenting agreement has not been made willingly. It may need revision if it is to survive.

■ In the long term, parents need to be prepared to change arrangements, even arrangements they themselves are comfortable with, in order to keep them comfortable for children. Children grow and change. Plans that suit a toddler may not suit him at all when he is four years old and starting school, while routines for a child just starting middle school may need to change several times in her first year to accommodate her new independence and peer group (see chapter 2).

Fathers and Mothers

When you are making—and remaking—parenting plans, it's important to believe and hang on to the fact that mothers and fathers can share equally in everything that matters most about being a parent—concern, responsibility, and reciprocated love for every child—without taking or vying for equal shares of their time.

Although more and more fathers in intact couples play a very big part in children's daily lives, very few—less than 10 percent—become the resident parents of their children after family breakdown. There are all kinds of reasons and composites of reasons why this is so, ranging from unrealistic but still pervasive conventions about divisions of family labor (Dad earns, Mom cares) to down-to-earth practicalities about working hours and schools.

Fathers often press for more contact, and especially for overnight visits from children, not because they actually want that extra time right now but because they fear that they will otherwise lose (or fail to build) a close relationship with their children after the separation. Research strongly suggests that this particular fear is groundless. The quality of contact—parent and child looking forward to seeing each other and having fun together—is far more important than its quantity, and for all but the youngest children, frequent communication, in all available forms (video-messaging, e-mail, and text, as well as phone, letters, and postcards) thickens up the parent-child relationship between physical meetings.

DAYTIME-ONLY CONTACT DOES NOT REDUCE ATTACHMENT

Overnight care in early infancy does not appear to determine attachment security with the second parent. Warm, lively, attuned care-giving interactions between baby and the second parent appear to be what is central to the growth of attachment security in that relationship.

Source: McIntosh 2011

FATHERS IN SOLE CHARGE

Recent American research shows that:

- One-third of fathers with working wives are a regular source of child care for their children; this figure is higher in some nonwhite families.
- The number of dads regularly caring for their children increased from 26 percent in 2002 to 32 percent in 2010.
- Among fathers with preschoolers in 2010, 20 percent were primary caregivers.
- The number of stay-at-home dads increased by 50 percent between 2003 and 2006.

Source: American Psychological Association 2013

If the arrangements you make for your children's lives after family breakdown are to optimize their security and well-being, they must reflect or at least take account of their lives when you were all together. Within many separating couples, involvement and concern (as well as love) for a child is mutual, but one parent is better able than the other to manifest that concern as practical caring. In the early years especially, the prior relationship between parent and child, and the extent to which it has been hands-on, is critical to future planning. Although the numbers of fathers taking an active part in their children's care is increasing rapidly, it is still the case that, irrespective of what either of them might have preferred, many more mothers

Mother of boy, aged eight months
"I'd trust him absolutely to do what's necessary for Liam, but I wouldn't trust him to do, or even to wonder, what Liam will enjoy the most."

Girl, aged seven
"I get mixed up about who's picking me up and where I'm going. My teacher tries to help. I think she has stuff about it written down. But I don't like it; don't like it that I don't know who to look for . . . that's why I was crying when he came yesterday. Not 'cause he was late or 'cause I didn't want to go with him like my mom said but 'cause I wasn't sure it was going to be him or who."

Girl, aged twelve, with a sister, aged three

"It was too far and cost too much for Daddy to come to see us for the day, so we had to go for weekends. Staying with him at the beginning was really sort of scary. He'd made a room for us which was OK-ish but no nightlight and he hadn't bought the kind of food Amelia ever eats (he'd got pork chops for dinner and no dessert or cookies), and he sort of didn't know how to look after her—or after me either. He'd bathed Amelia and put her to bed lots of times, and so he did that OK but then he came downstairs leaving her wide awake in a strange room, and I had to take her for a pee and stay while she settled. Luckily, I'd been allowed to babysit her sometimes since my birthday, so she was used to me taking care of her at night. But in the morning she was awake long before Dad (and long before I usually get up on weekends), so I had to wake up too and help her find clothes and get dressed and everything, and it just didn't feel like there was anybody but me in charge."

than fathers have been children's principal caregivers since they were born.

You may not be one of these, but there are still many men, including truly loving fathers, who have never changed that proverbial diaper and would be at a loss if left for more than half a day in sole charge of a baby or toddler. This is one of the better reasons why fewer fathers than mothers become the resident parent.

Even with older children, a father who has not played much of a part in the practical details of their lives while the family was intact may struggle to keep them safe, secure, and happy if he is suddenly left to cope alone. If you do not know the name of your eight-year-old's best friend (this week) or teacher (this semester), you'll have to climb to the top of a very steep learning curve before she is likely to be happy with you picking her up from school for an overnight.

You can learn, now, what you did not feel the need to know before, and children who love you will help. But the learning may take time. So both of you need to think honestly and realistically about what the sharing arrangements you are considering adopting immediately will actually be like for each of your children. Are they the arrangements that will best maximize each child's happiness in this unhappy situation, irrespective of your adult convenience, or are they the arrangements that best suit you two or that strike you as "fair"?

While there are some fathers who are not competent as care-givers when they are in sole charge of very young children, there are some mothers who are not competent either. It can't be taken for granted that being almost entirely with the mother as pri-mary caregiver will make a child happier now or be better for his attachment security and positive adjustment in the future. Being a lone parent is extraordinarily different from being a part-nered one, and even mothers who feel that their ex played little part in the children's lives before the separation sometimes have trouble coping when they find themselves on their own. If such a mother also has a history of mental illness or depression, or if she is battling depression for the first time now, the stress of being left with almost unrelieved and solitary child care may reduce the quality of her relationship with the child and the care she can give. Provided the father's motivation and intentions are good, he is emotionally and physically available to the child, and her safety with him is not in question, having her spend time with him may be valuable to all concerned, even if his parenting is not conventionally competent.

SHARED PARENTING USUALLY MEANS shared resources, of which money and housing are the most immediately important (see pp. 75–76 and pp. 86–91). It's commonplace—almost expected—for separating parents to quarrel over these things, but before you get involved, or let your legal advisers get you embroiled, take time to think about how much these adult-sounding issues can affect your children. Any arrangement that leaves one of you much poorer than the other can seriously jeopardize the poorer parent's opportunities for a loving, caring relationship with the children, and can even deprive children of contact.

Either parent may end up on the losing side of a division of already-scarce resources. Mothers' financial situations often nosedive after separation because their ex-husbands cannot or will not pay anything approaching adequate maintenance and their own earnings are inadequate or even threatened. Some women who continue to work full-time after separation nevertheless find it impossible to run what was a family home on their single wage. And some women have to give up work once they are on their own because their hours, their earnings, and the costs of child care do not balance. Sudden household poverty can drain children's lives of accustomed pleasures. Even those who are old enough to understand that you are broke rather than mean are liable to resent your sudden refusal to let them go on school trips, continue with out-of-school music or judo classes, or dole out their accustomed pocket money.

Fathers, perhaps especially fathers who are trying hardest to behave decently when their families break up, are just as likely to be left relatively poor, and where housing is concerned, it is often fathers who suffer most. If the family was already struggling to meet mortgage and utility payments, divorce may be a final straw. If the whole family has to move out and find alternative accommodations, welfare will ensure some (basic) kind of housing for the mother and children but not for the father. He has become a single man with financial commitments that he may not be able to meet and who may be left literally homeless.

Girl, aged nine
"Spring break with Daddy was kind of like camping. I slept on a mat and there was funny food and not much showering. It was really fun."

If the separating couple is better off, the father may move out of the family home and leave the mother and children in it; however, unless he is notably well-off, it may be difficult, even impossible, for him to finance a second place to live where the children can comfortably visit. A room may be the best such a father can afford, and even if he moves into an apartment, the chances of both parental homes being equally child-friendly are very small. If your new home is notably less comfortable than the family home you have left, your ex—or you yourself—

SHARED PARENTING AND POVERTY

"Concern about the effects of child support enforcement on the fathers themselves has been minimal," acknowledges a team of prominent researchers headed by Irwin Garfinkel. But these effects have often been severe. Set by rigid formulae and often collected by garnisheeing wages, child-support payments often work great hardship on lower-income fathers. Urban Institute researcher Elaine Sorensen observes that bureaucratically established child-support orders often exceed poor fathers' ability to pay. Worse, she complains, when divorced fathers lose their jobs, have their wages or hours cut, or become sick or disabled, they find it very hard to get their child-support obligation adjusted accordingly. "The process for adjusting [child-support] orders is quite bureaucratic . . . According to U.S. Census data, only 4 percent of noncustodial fathers who were paying child support under an order received a downward adjustment when their earnings fell by more than 15 percent between one year and the next." Such numbers give substance to analyst John Smith's criticism that "get tough" child-support measures are "running [poor fathers] into poverty and homelessness."

Should a divorced father fall into arrears in paying child support, he may lose his driver's license, his business license, or his professional license, even if the loss of his license deprives him of the ability to pay off the amount in arrears. One divorced father whose legal fight over visitation and support payments left him so penniless that he had to live in a tent in the Santa Cruz Mountains vehemently protested, "I have less rights that a damn criminal in jail."

Source: The Howard Center for Family, Religion, and Society,
The Family in America, online edition

may feel that it is not suitable for a baby or safe for a toddler, while older children will inevitably regret, even resent, moving between the two places, however eager they are to spend time with both people. If a child visits reluctantly, his time with you will do little to build your relationship and may actually make it more difficult to maintain.

However mutual your parenting, you cannot stretch a tight budget further than it can reach, but you can resist scoring over

Father of boy, aged six
"I wanted equal time as a parent, and my ex went along with it because it meant she was only a single mother part-time. But the truth is that by the time I'd paid rent for the apartment and maintenance to her for the kid, I was too broke to give Eric a great time. I couldn't afford lots of trips and days out; the place was cramped, there wasn't a yard, and he didn't have any friends nearby. I knew he'd rather be at home with his mom and his friends, and who could blame him?"

each other financially or listening to lawyers telling you what you are entitled to instead of relying on your own sense of what will make the best of a bad job. If you are both trying to support each other's parenting so that the children can benefit from it, an equal distribution of what's available is much more meaningfully fair than equal shares of children's time.

PUTTING YOUR PARENTING PLAN INTO ACTION

Which of you is the resident parent and which the nonresident does affect tax and welfare matters but will affect your parenting plans only if you cannot agree on your roles and therefore have to seek legal intervention. Provided you agree, you can make whatever arrangements you please for the children. Unless they are considered to be at risk, nobody is interested in whether or not the children actually spend the stated alternate weekends and one night in the week with the nonresident parent.

The smooth running of contact between your children and their nonresident parent depends on both of you accepting your own and each other's different formal roles and both being firmly committed to continuing contact at all costs. The most helpful stance you, as resident parent, can adopt is as an active and proactive supporter of the relationship between each of your children and their nonresident mom or dad, not only practically but also in the emotional sense of expecting and encouraging children to enjoy it. Perhaps only someone who has seen their excited child off on an expedition with the other parent, so eager for the "hello hug" that she forgets a good-bye one, can understand how difficult that can be. But given that you could not all stay contentedly together as a family, this is the very best you can do and in the long run of your child's development, worth any amount of effort. If your effort is to pay off, your ex also needs to be active and proactive over contact. Being active means taking a full part in planning and making arrangements for the children and then sticking to them—cheerfully. Being proactive means finding different ways of having good times with the children and being alert to any problems and eager to discuss them.

However hard you are each trying, though, minor difficulties with contact ar-

> **Mother of two boys, aged eight and nine**
> "I love my time with the kids. I get through the working week for those weekends with them. But I hate picking them up and taking them back 'cause it seems I can't do anything right. I try very hard not to be late, but with the buses, it can happen, and you should hear him if I'm early . . . I try to do things with the boys that he'll approve of, like swimming, but last time we did that it turned out that Felix had had an ear infection and wasn't supposed to go in the water. He hadn't told me that, but that didn't stop him calling me irresponsible in front of them both. As for food: you'd never think I'd been the one who shopped and cooked for them for seven years. He quizzes me about what they've had so I feel I should be writing out menus. It can't really be that he doesn't trust me: I'm a good mom and always have been. So the truth is he doesn't want me to have them; maybe he hopes I'll drop out."

rangements are inevitable, especially at the beginning. Whether you are the resident or the contact parent, you are human and under tremendous stress. You can forget things (that swimming gear, *again*), be late for pickup or drop-off, seem grumpy or disapproving of the other parent, or strain your parenting plan by allowing or encouraging a child to behave in ways the other parent has vetoed (too much TV). The great majority of contact problems are of this kind. They are the kinds of niggle that are normal within most intact marriages and, given mutual goodwill, easily overlooked or dealt with by compromise. It is when

DRIFTING AWAY FROM CONTACT WITH ABSENT PARENTS

In an American sample of more than 11,000 children, two-thirds of separated fathers were consistent, over time, in their contact with their children, whether they were highly or rarely involved. However, almost a quarter of separated fathers were not consistent, but started with frequent contact, which gradually dwindled to nothing.

High levels of father involvement were more likely when children were older at the time of separation and were more likely to be maintained when fathers and mothers lived close to each other.

Separated mothers were more likely to be highly involved with their children and much less likely to drift out of contact.

Source: Cheadle, Amato, and King 2010

goodwill is lacking that minor difficulties escalate into conflicts that can threaten contact itself.

When contact is difficult to arrange so that children are often kept on tenterhooks and sometimes disappointed, or if visits are more or less miserable and children are reluctant, it's all too easy for one or both parents to decide that the children would be better off without it, or simply to let it dwindle and lapse. Easy, but wrong. A very large body of research says that there are no circumstances in which it is better for a child to lose touch with a parent after family breakdown or eventual divorce. There are many different types of contact. If one really cannot be made to work, try another.

Overnight Contact—Ages and Circumstances

Most contact arrangements include overnight stays, often one or two weekend nights at a time and sometimes some holiday nights also. It is overnight contact that causes most problems both for parents and for children. When it works well, there are major advantages over day visits, notably that the child has the opportunity to "live with" the contact parent; that the two of them have a base rather than having to spend their time together visiting relatives or friends, making expeditions, or wandering aimlessly around the park; and that the contact parent cares for the child through every minute and aspect of his or her way of being.

> **Girl, aged four**
> "Do you know Daddy wears glasses in the night and contact lenses in the day? I saw him put them in . . ."

However, shared parenting that includes overnight stays may be impossible because of one parent's accommodation or lack of it, and even when it is practically possible, it does not always work well from children's point of view. Separating couples need to face up honestly to the possibility that at this time overnights will not work. Problems include a particular child being too young; one or the other household having inadequate income or housing; and one or the other parent being unable to provide appropriate care, having too long and too inflexible working hours, or living at too great a distance.

Sleepovers for Babies and Toddlers

Staying overnight with the contact parent does not only mean that the child has to go to and settle in an unaccustomed place but also, of course, that he must leave the resident parent and the home setup in order to do so. The younger the child, the more likely it is that the leaving element—leaving Mom and home—will be stressful. As suggested earlier, overnight stays for babies and toddlers should not be taken for granted (see chapter 1). They may work well for all concerned if the parents were both accustomed to caring for the child while the family was intact and the child is closely attached to both, and they may be helpful overall if the resident parent badly needs respite, but generally speaking regular and frequent nights away should be planned for with care and caution, especially if the child is three years old or less.

If you do decide to include overnight stays with the nonresident parent in your parenting plan for a baby or toddler, it may

OVERNIGHT CARE FOR CHILDREN OF PARENTS LIVING APART, PART 1

A think tank convened by the U.S. Association of Family and Conciliation Courts (AFCC) ("Closing the Gap: Research, Policy, Practice, and Shared Parenting") and the two-part paper that followed it have advanced research in this contentious area. An important area of consensus is that post-divorce care arrangements should take account of both early attachment formation and joint parental involvement rather than focusing on one or the other.

There are five studies comparing the outcomes of different patterns of shared care for very young children, including overnights with the nonresident parent. Because their samples, data sources, and analyzed variables differ, they cannot be evidentially grouped. However, consensus was reached on one point: "The small group of relevant studies to date substantiates caution about high frequency overnight time schedules in the 0–3 year period, particularly when the child's security with a parent is unformed, or parents cannot agree on how to share care of the child . . . [but] cautions against any overnight care in the first three years have not been supported."

Source: Pruett, McIntosh, and Kelly 2014

be quite difficult to be sure how these are affecting him. You and his father will both need to put yourself in his small shoes in order to understand. A one- or two-year-old who is going for an overnight stay is not old enough to understand the plan or to anticipate how long he will be away, so although he may well be distressed at the point of separation from you, he'll be no more distressed than if he was going to Dad for the afternoon. Once that mini-parting is over, he is misleadingly likely to appear to settle with his father in the new place, and it is only when he is returned home and reunited with you that the full extent of any upset will become clear. It is usually *the mother's relationship* with the child that is vulnerable to too-early separations, and you are the one who will bear the brunt of his clingy and unsettled behavior.

The fact that your baby or toddler seems happily settled while he is away with his dad and very obviously unsettled when he

OVERNIGHT CARE FOR CHILDREN OF PARENTS LIVING APART, PART 2: TURNING THEORY INTO PRACTICE

This companion piece to Part 1 is a guide to decision making about infant overnight care, principally directed to the family court community but useful also to parents. AFCC research emphasizes that "parenting orders or plans for children 0–3 years should foster both developmental security and the health of each parent-child relationship, now and into the future," and charts recommended frequencies of overnights from "rare or no overnights" through one to four per month and five-plus per month against a list of considerations.

"Rare or no overnights" should be considered if a child:

- Is not safe with both parents or the parents with each other.
- Does not have an established trusting relationship of at least six months with the nonresident parent.
- Has needs to which the parent is not sensitive.
- Has special needs (including continuing breast-feeding) that are not supported in proposed arrangements.
- Over three to four weeks shows signs of stress such as irritability, excessive clinging on separation, frequent crying, aggressive or self-harming behavior, regression in established behaviors such as toileting, low persistence in play and learning.
- Has parents who live an unmanageable distance apart.
- Has a parent who cannot personally care for the child overnight but must use child care.

Source: McIntosh, Pruett, and Kelly 2014

comes back to you may easily mislead you both. Your ex, understandably, may feel that he is doing fine because the baby was happy with him and the overnight was stress-free. Something you did must have caused the child's unusual behavior when it was over. You, equally understandably, may feel that the baby's father is to blame—perhaps for letting him stay up too late or watch too much TV—and you may resent the fact that stress-free visits for him always mean a stressful couple of days for you.

————

THE RESEARCH INFORMATION noted in the boxes in this section was gathered for very large groups of children from many different families. It does not mean that staying with Dad overnight should be ruled out for your particular baby or toddler or that it will certainly be appropriate for your individual four-year-old. Your children and your environments are all unique. The mix of your relationships, your ex's relationships, all your temperaments, needs, and circumstances may be a recipe that makes any contact arrangement stressful for the child or makes it supportive. You may find helpful a new online education program, Young Children in Divorce and Separation (YCIDS), specifically for separated parents. What the research information does mean is that if you are making contact arrangements for a baby, toddler, or preschool child, you need to consider questions such as the following very carefully before you settle on frequent overnight stays:

What is the child's existing relationship with her father? Leaving you in order to stay with Daddy overnight is unlikely to be upsetting if he was her primary or equal caregiver before the separation, or if he is entirely accustomed to caring for her and she demonstrates her attachment to him by readily turn-

---

**YOUNG CHILDREN IN DIVORCE AND SEPARATION (YCIDS):
AN ONLINE PROGRAM FOR PARENTS**

YCIDS is a ninety-minute online education program for separated parents of very young children. YCIDS simplifies complex research, supporting parents to better understand early development, and to better manage co-parenting of very young children, between two homes. Parents can complete it at home, or as part of a divorce mediation or court process.

Source: http://www.familytransitions.com.au/
Family_Transitions/Parent_Resources.html

---

ing to him when she needs reassurance or comfort. However, if hands-on parenting of this child will be more or less new to them both, overnights with the father should ideally wait until some months of daytime contact have helped them to build a relationship.

Can her father provide constant personal care while the child is with him? If he will need to go out to work or to socialize and plans to employ a babysitter, he is not in a position to have such a young child stay with him. However, if the child has a caregiver at home—a nanny, au pair, or babysitter—who can go with her for overnights, this may be a good arrangement.

Are there older siblings who will regularly and frequently stay overnight with their father? If so, it may be difficult to arrange separate daytime contact for the youngest child and seem better for everyone if all the children go together (see pp. 53–55).

Could you start with one night at a time rather than two, and alternate weekends rather than every weekend? The more frequent and the longer overnight stays are, the more stress they tend to put on a child.

Do you have urgent practical reasons for wanting this child to be away from home overnight? If you have mental or physical health problems or are suffering from stress or exhaustion, overnight breaks can help you to maintain the quality of your parenting. However, if separating from you to stay with her father is, in the event, unmanageably stressful for the child, any respite her absence might give you will be lost because it is on her return home and in her relationship with you that anxious, unsettled, clingy, or aggressive behavior will show itself.

Will both of you be alert to changes in the baby or toddler's behavior after he returns home from overnight contact? Such changes may reflect real and lasting disturbance to her development rather than a temporary upset. It is enormously important that even the youngest child sees the contact parent regularly, but how that is arranged is equally important.

Overnight Visits for Older Children

Although it would be idiotic to suggest that a child of three or under may be better off without overnight contact but becomes ready for it on his fourth birthday, these research studies do strongly suggest that staying away overnight becomes less difficult at around that age.

School-aged children are far less likely to find leaving Mom and home for a night or two highly stressful in itself. Their attachment is developed and, hopefully, secure, and their ability to understand plans and anticipate reunion is dawning if not yet complete. Furthermore, many of them are becoming accustomed to sleepovers with friends, which means not only that they are accustomed to being away from you but also that they are used to sleeping in a different bed in another house. For these older children, what matters most of all is that spending time with the nonresident parent, and staying overnight with him or her, is a pleasure, in prospect and in fact. Of course this mostly depends on the relationship between them and on issues dealt with earlier, such as whether or not the child will be with siblings and where and how the

Boy, aged nine

"It's since I started going to my dad's on weekends that I've really started swimming. We go to a great big pool, and he comes in with me to swim, and then I get a swimming lesson. Last week the teacher said I'm doing well, and this week I'm moving up a group."

OVERNIGHT CONTACT FOR FOUR- AND FIVE-YEAR-OLDS

The vast majority of variations between overnight care groups in the four- to five-year-old age group were accounted for by factors other than overnight care patterns, with particular emphasis on the impact of inter-parental conflict and lack of warmth in parenting on children's self-regulating capacities at this stage.

Source: McIntosh et al. 2010

contact parent lives. However, there are other points that may be important to smooth-running contact that is satisfactory for the child, no matter how difficult it may be for one or both parents.

- Being not only allowed but also encouraged to look forward to the contact times. You can easily turn pleasurable anticipation into guilt by denigrating the father or bemoaning your loneliness when the child is away (see chapter 6).
- Feeling able to talk to one parent about time spent with the other but never being pressured to do so or asked to carry messages between the two.
- Having arrangements with a balanced mixture of regularity and flexibility. A child will not look forward to a weekend with Dad if she will be missing her best friend's birthday party.
- Having the contact parent's full-time attention. Arriving for the weekend to find that Dad has to work on Saturday is a letdown, no matter what kind of care he has arranged to cover his absence. Equally, the child wants to spend time with his father, not with his father's friends or his girlfriend, so extra adults are usually unwelcome (see chapter 3).
- Something fun to do with the parent. Overnight visits work best when the child gets to do something with Dad that he really enjoys and doesn't otherwise get to do regularly.
- Being able to keep in contact with home life during contact visits. Children should be free to call or text the other parent and to do so privately if they wish. For older children in particular, contact with friends may be overwhelmingly important. A child who texts or goes on social media from home should not need special permission to do so when with the other parent. A spare phone charger to keep there and perhaps the gift of extra minutes will help to prevent her from feeling cut off (see chapter 4).
- With school the next morning, Sunday evenings are often rushed and stressful even when children have been at home all weekend; having been away, combined with the

transition from one parent to another, can make things worse. To keep Sundays calm, children need to feel comfortable fulfilling school commitments during weekend visits. There must be time, encouragement, and a suitable place to do homework, study for a test, or practice for an upcoming performance.

Teenagers often find regular weekend contact very difficult even if parents allow some flexibility. Both of you need to accept that a young person's peer group may matter more to her than either parent (at least at a conscious level). She wants to be where her friends will—or can—be, so unless the parents live in the same area, she is not likely to want to go away very often.

Most young people are very bad at making plans in advance. Your teenager will not be able to choose which weekends he can be away without missing anything that matters to him because he will not know what he will be doing when. And it is useless to pressure him to decide because he has no idea what his friends will be doing when, either. The chances are that none of them will be doing anything adults recognize as special (and can therefore put in a calendar). What they will be doing is hanging out.

Encouraging a teenager to invite friends to come with her may help to keep up her enthusiasm for weekends with the nonresident parent, especially if his or her area or home offers something interesting (such as proximity to an important sports stadium or a seaside location). She may not accept, though. However much a visit has to offer, she may not want to mix friends from one home and parent with the other.

The only thing that really matters about contact is that the child and the parent spend enjoyable time together. If your teenager no longer enjoys regular weekends or even resents the pressure to go on with them, her father or mother might offer to meet up with her for dinner and a movie in her home area or to rendezvous in the nearest town. Any such suggestion will make it clear that the parent is eager to see her on whatever terms she finds comfortable.

Handling Handovers

Whether they are going out for an afternoon, a weekend, or a week's vacation, most children—especially very young ones—find the actual transition from the care of one parent to the care of the other confusing and stressful. The more often such a transition is made (and the less well the parents manage it), the more disturbing the contact arrangement is.

- Make sure your child passes rapidly and seamlessly (or better still, with a couple of minutes of overlap) from your care to her father's (or via a third party if necessary). Even a moment when she's not sure which parent is in charge of her may be enough to make her panicky.
- If you and your ex can't manage to meet and be friendly, even for five minutes, don't have your child wait for Daddy alone at the front gate feeling that nobody's in charge of her. Use an intermediary instead, dropping her off with somebody she knows and likes from whose home Daddy can pick her up.
- She must be allowed to take special precious possessions back and forth with her. A baby's special blanket or teddy is obvious, but her older brother's old-fashioned, illuminated, and loudly ticking clock may be almost as important to him at bedtime.

SWAPPING FROM THE CARE OF ONE PARENT TO THE OTHER

A study of overnight care by Solomon and George (1999) identified "frequent transitions of care between parents who remain acrimonious and struggle to facilitate a smooth transition for the infant" as adding to the difficulties.

Source: McIntosh 2011

- Make the changeover positive: she needs to be sure that you want her to go, her father wants her to come, and you're both certain that she'll have a great time.

- Keep the actual parting brief. Don't tell her *again* how much you'll miss her or revisit plans and arrangements that have already been discussed. "I love you. See you tomorrow" is enough.

Daytime Contact and Geography

Seeing the contact parent during daytime rather than overnight visits suits a lot of children, especially the very young. If parents live close to each other and their parenting is at least polite if not mutual (see chapter 5), daytime contact is so easy that overnight or weekend visiting that is genuinely for everyone's pleasure often develops out of it.

> **Twin girl and boy, aged four**
> "We like having sleepovers with our dad, don't we, Tom? But you always have to go home in the middle of the night, don't you? And then I have to go, too."

As the twins quoted here grew older, they began to choose which household they would be in on any particular day, and by the time they left elementary school, they could (and often did) walk between the two homes. They had a bedroom as well as a parent in each.

From children's points of view, that is an ideal to aspire to, but it is not one that many couples will achieve, because living close together with a lot of popping in and out going on is not what most people who are separating or divorcing want. Even if they don't want to see each other, though, parents who want the children to see both of them need to recognize that geography is crucial (see chapter 4), because living close to each other is what will make that possible. What is more, if being with Dad on weekends often starts with him driving them to their Saturday activities, and he always does something with them during school breaks or maybe even on snow days, children are more likely to feel that being with him is an integral part of their daily lives rather than something special and separate.

If the two of you live far apart, visits will cost a lot of money—in fares or gas—and time, and a few hours with the child may not be enough to make the journey seem worthwhile for your ex or the resultant freedom worthwhile for you. Furthermore, it is really difficult to have a fun time with a child with-

> **Mother of three children, separated for two years**
>
> "I regret the contact now. I wish I'd broken it completely. I don't think he'd have bothered taking me to court if I'd said no. I thought the kids needed a link with him—and maybe they do—but their contact with him has been so erratic that they've never known if he was coming or not, and that's probably been more damaging than if they'd just never seen him."

out a base to go to. Playing ball in the park is fine while the sun shines and the child's energy runs high, but what if it pours with rain and he is tired? Under those circumstances "ordinary" families go home, and a young child will not fully understand why Dad and he cannot.

Whether you have decided to stick with daytime contact because your child is too young for sleeping away or because the father's accommodation isn't suitable for overnight stays, this is a fragile kind of contact, which all too often deteriorates and then fades away. Since nothing apart from losing both parents is more damaging to a child than having one parent vanish out of her life, it is worth considering some ways of making daytime contact with a parent who doesn't live nearby easier and more lasting:

- Could you, the resident parent, allow your ex to use your and the child's own home as a base for visits? If you don't want to see your ex, you could go out for the afternoon. If you can't bear the idea of him being in the house alone as if it was still his, would your mother or a friend agree to be there?

- If your home is completely out of bounds, is there a relative or friend whom you trust and the child knows and likes who would let them meet in her house?
- Does the child already spend occasional nights with grandparents or other relatives who live locally? If so, could father visit the child there?
- Is there an indoor activity center that your child enjoys to which you could drive her to meet and spend time with her father who would then bring her home?

For older children and teenagers, daytime visits between weekends or vacations may be the more valuable because of the effort they cost the contact parent. The children will know that if Dad takes all that trouble to get to the school drama production or the teacher-parent consultation evening or an important swim meet, he really cares about their lives.

Sometimes these visits can take place without the parents meeting each other: a school play often has two or three performances, and parents could therefore go separately. A concert is a one-off, though, and so is a sports event or a school consultation, so although attending such functions together may not be something you discussed when you were first making parenting plans, it is an issue that eventually needs to be addressed. Teenage or student accomplishments often involve public performance or acknowledgment. Is one of you always going to miss the days when your child most wants you to be proud of him—such as a school awards ceremony or university graduation? And what about the opposite kind of day when he needs a parent's presence and support: Will only one of you answer a call from the police station or even the emergency room?

Supervised Daytime Visits

Sometimes a mother really does not want her children to see their father at all, even for brief daytime visits. Her ex cannot insist on seeing the children against her wishes, but neither can she prevent him just because that is what she would prefer (see pp. 124–29). Sometimes a father is so intimidated by an angry ex that he backs off, and the children are deprived of contact with him, but if a lawyer, a mediator, or a social worker is involved, it will become clear to the mother that she really cannot keep the children from seeing their father without a reason to which the family court would pay attention. Such a reason can only be to do with the children's safety—such as believing that the children might be at risk with him; that his present environment would be unsafe or a bad influence on them; that they might be exposed to alcoholism, drug addiction, or mental illness; or that, given the opportunity, the father would abduct the children out of her care and possibly out of the country.

If the two parents cannot sort out the question of the father's access between them, then the matter should go to court quickly so that as little time as possible elapses before regular contact is established or re-established. Although he may not realize it, the father can apply for a contact order (see pp. 91–100). Once an application has been made, parents are in the court's hands. It will make an order if it thinks that is in the child's best interests, but it may not be the order they expected or would have chosen. Child protection is the court's priority so the mother's concerns will be carefully listened to; but the court recognizes the importance to children of contact with both parents and will therefore try to balance the two. The court's best available compromise is often weekly or biweekly daytime visits that are supervised by an approved third party—sometimes a grandparent or other relative at her home. Most mothers are indignant that any contact is being ordered against her expressed wishes; most fathers find compulsory supervision of their brief time with the children deeply insulting. But however inadequate such meetings may be, both to the children's needs and to their father's, supervised contact is better than no contact at all, and the arrangement will usually be temporary. If all goes well, the nonresident parent can apply after a few months to have contact liberalized.

Contact from a Distance

In this era of increasingly sophisticated communications, parents and children can stay in touch with each other even when they cannot spend time together; it's important to realize how much this can help their relationships, even when practical circumstances are against them. The point of regular and frequent contact with the nonresident parent is to assure children that although he is no longer physically present in their home, their father is still their father and as loving, interested, and concerned for them as ever. And when children are with the father on vacation, they similarly need to know that although they are away from their mother, she is still there for them. However desperately an absent parent misses being with a child in person—talking and listening, hugging and holding hands, playing games and washing faces—he or she can give this assurance in words and pictures, provided they are the right ones. Not all the right words and pictures will be high-tech. Most children love getting mail and will be thrilled with letters, provided they are typed so that a child who can read at all can read them privately rather than having them read to her, and provided the absent parent doesn't expect a long screed in return. Picture postcards are fun to get and keep—your child might like an album to collect them in—and sending one back requires only a few written words. A weekly card could show where Daddy has been or something he's seen (OK, you're still in Portland, Maine, like last week, like always, but this is a different bus!), and you could give your child a supply of stamped, addressed postcards to send back.

The phone is an obvious channel of communication but sometimes expensive—especially if you are on different continents—and not always very comfortable for children under about five. Younger ones may love to answer the phone when it rings but often find it very difficult to listen to what the caller is saying and then reply. If your child is comfortable using a phone, you might consider giving him a cell phone rather earlier than you would have if the family had stayed intact, so that he knows he can call you to make arrangements or to chat, and do so privately. Some children find it difficult to talk in front of Mom or in front of siblings. Older children are usually inseparable from their cells, which means that you can reach out to them at almost any time. Being called is disruptive, though. You obviously shouldn't call your child during the school day, and you won't want her trying to call you when you are in a meeting. The solution is texting, and today's children become exceedingly competent at sending texts and at reading them at a surprisingly early age. If by any chance you haven't yet found a need for this particular skill, teach yourself now.

If there is a computer available and a resident parent who will help, Skype (and a growing number of similar videophone services) has a lot more to offer all ages than an ordinary phone. You need to sign up, but subscribing doesn't cost anything and calls are free however far apart you are and however long they last. A teenage friend in LA completed a series of chemistry practice papers on Skype with her dad in Australia. Video calls are especially valuable to the very young, though, because you and your child can see each other. That's enormously important if you have to be away from a very small child for days or even weeks at a time because it will help her to hang on to a clear image of you (and you to keep track of her growing up). A somewhat older child can show you the gap where her tooth came out or his first big boy's haircut. If the cameras are properly adjusted at either end, you can even show picture books and read stories.

E-mails are also invaluable, not only for words but for sharing photos. If you are apart, and whether your child uses a laptop, a smartphone, or a tablet, it will probably be worth getting her an e-mail address of her own. If you plan to write to her a lot, make sure that she will check her e-mail often.

Social networking sites such as Facebook keep millions of people in touch with one another, but children should not use them until they are thirteen years old, and even then may not want a parent potentially mixed up with their peers. If your child has a smartphone, he can use its camera to take pictures of things he wants to show you, e-mail them to you, and get an immediate voice or voicemail reaction. That isn't social networking, but it's certainly contact.

8

When Contact Fails

Everybody who is professionally involved with parents who are separating—such as researchers, social workers, lawyers, and family court judges—takes the view that it is in children's best interests to be in regular contact with both parents, the non-resident parent as well as the parent they live with, and that it is parents' responsibility to make sure that they do. This book goes somewhat further. What it calls "separating better" is largely concerned with the relationships parents can make with each other, and the parenting plans they can put in place to ensure not just that the children stay in contact with them both but that they both go on being mother or father to them.

Problems around contact are inevitable, and commonplace ones that contribute to "separating worse" have been dealt with in earlier chapters. But the ultimate problem, fortunately not at all commonplace, is not just difficulties around contact between child and nonresident parent but absolute refusal of it. That is the subject of this chapter.

WILLING PARENT AND RELUCTANT CHILD

Contact with both parents is a child's right and is not the parents' right. The welfare and best interests of a child are the most important of a court's considerations and the wishes and feelings of children are part of that. However, that doesn't mean that children can choose whether to have contact with a parent or not. How much, if any, notice is taken of children's feelings or choices theoretically depends on their age and level of understanding but, in practice, also depends on the individual professionals who are involved in a particular case. There is no set age at which a child's wishes will be taken into account by a court, but it is unlikely that attention will be paid to the views of very young children, as they are thought to be too immature to understand and make decisions about contact. The views of older children—especially teenagers—may be taken more seriously but, in the eyes of some resident parents, are often not taken seriously enough. Courts take the view that unless there is an officially recognized child protection issue, it is the responsibility of parents to encourage their child to take part in contact *whatever the child's feelings about the matter.*

Mother of girl, aged fourteen
"She really doesn't like seeing him. Really hates going to that community center place and sitting and talking to him. But still she has to go every three weeks, and I have to take her. If I didn't, I'd be in breach of a court order. They could even send me to prison, I think."

No child is old enough to voice a decision about contact if that means choosing which of his parents he prefers to live with or how much time he wants to spend with each. No child should even be asked to make such agonizing choices, especially knowing that everything he says will be shared with both parents. But no child who can speak fluently is too young to express his feelings about seeing the nonresident parent, and these should certainly be heard—as they are when a full assessment of the family dynamics and patterns of attachment are made—and fed into the court's adult decision making. Unfortunately, such assessments are not always ordered, or when they are ordered they are not always carried out by relevantly trained professionals.

Many parents say that when their child resisted seeing the parent she didn't live with, they found themselves in double trouble. When contact had been ordered by the court, or had been arranged in mediation and would come to court if it didn't work out, they were held responsible for making it happen, and if it didn't happen, they were held to blame. Convincing a mediator or social worker that she had done her best to get the child to contact but the child really refused to go did not get a resident parent off the hook. On the contrary, it was assumed that if the child completely rejected contact with the other parent it could only be because the resident parent had put her off (see pp. 124–29).

The Family Justice Council has recently recommended that young people should participate more fully in the court process by, for example, writing to the judge or even seeing him. But many professionals in divorce work are against this practice.

WHEN DID YOU LAST SEE YOUR FATHER?

"Children often make allegations about their parents which are not credible; children can feel unable to express their view or may even be unable to form their own view of a matter so their expressed wishes and feelings may be misleading.

"A child may express the view that s/he does not wish to see their parent; this view may reflect a negative view of the nonresident parent by the parent with day to day care which may be reinforced by that parent's immediate circle of family and friends. Sometimes other professionals are also enlisted by the resident parent who may, for example, tell a GP or school that the child suffers from stomach cramps, headaches or bedwetting prior to visits with the other parent."

Source: Kirkland Weir 2009

Contact with a nonresident parent works best when child and parent look forward to seeing each other and enjoy being together. If that has never been the case for your family, or if it was the case for a while but the child has now begun to protest about visits and say that he doesn't want to go, don't let the situation drag on, as the more time passes since child and parent spent time together, the more reluctant the child will probably become. There are many reasons why children refuse contact, and it's important to come to understand, as quickly as possible, what kind of problem is putting your child off. Does it have to do with what he feels about the other parent, or does it have to do with what he feels about you (and leaving you)? Or is the problem something specific about the circumstances of his visits?

- Encourage your child to talk about what he feels about seeing the other parent. Even a four-year-old may be able to explain why he doesn't want to visit. Sometimes unwillingness to spend time with the other parent may hinge on specific things that can be changed and put right, such as always having to share the visit with the parent's future partner.

- Try not to let the child pick up on your own thoughts or feelings about the man who is your ex-partner but his current-and-forever dad. As we have seen, you don't have to intend to alienate a child to do so (see pp. 118–24). Children often refuse contact as a result of subtle messages about the parent they are supposed to visit that they have picked up from the parent they live with. If you are furiously angry and upset with your ex, it is really difficult for a child who lives with you and loves you to put your feelings aside and look forward to seeing and loving him. You may be able to make it possible for the child to love you both if you spell out to him in whatever way he is old enough to understand the difference between his father's partnership with you (which has failed and made you furious) and his parenting of the child, which hasn't failed and makes you happy (see chapter 5).

- Force yourself to face the fact that whether he shows it in conventional ways or not, your child is experiencing real grief at the loss not only of the parent who doesn't live with him anymore but also of the two of you together: his parents as he knew them. However hard you try, neither of you is the same parent (or the same person) as you were before the family broke up, and your child's rejection of the contact arranged for him may be part of a refusal to accept what feels to him so much of a second best.

- Understand that an agony of conflict and split loyalty is inevitable for your child. He loves you both yet every sign of love for one feels like disloyalty to the other. He may be unable to feel comfortable with the other parent because visits inevitably involve hugs, and hugs make him feel guilty about you.

- Recognize that your child's reactions to contact with his other parent are almost certainly linked to the relationship between the two of you, now, and will continue to be so. The better the relationship and the more mutual your parenting (see pp. 108–13), the less likely it is that a child will refuse contact. Conversely, the fact that your child is refusing contact suggests that the two of you are not on good terms or perhaps are not on terms at all. Do try to keep (or reinstate) some kind of communication with your ex so that the two of you can discuss what the real problem is and what is to be done about it.

Reasons for Children Refusing Contact

Handovers

If your child makes clear his refusal to take part in a visit with the nonresident parent even while it is only in prospect and hasn't yet begun, it may be that the very beginning is most of the problem. Maybe the child would be perfectly happy with his father once the two of them were together and without you. You can find out if that is the case only if you can manage the handover.

Whether children are collected from home or from a neutral place, or driven to the father's home or chosen meeting place, handover times are often the most difficult parts of contact visits for younger children, and even older children (who are expected to go of their own volition rather than be handed over) sometimes find the actual transition from one parent to the other very anxious-making, so some degree of difficulty is commonplace. As we have seen there are many ways you can help, from making the handover quick and smooth with no lingering good-byes, to dropping off or collecting a child from a neutral place such as school or a relative's house. However, if extreme problems with handover are part of a child's attempt to refuse contact altogether, such simple measures are unlikely to solve them.

Wherever you are trying to hand him over, a young child may adamantly refuse to leave you, clinging to your leg or your skirt and keeping his head buried so as not to see his father. If he is small enough, he could be (and some children are) literally "handed over," screaming and struggling. Although that may be a quick solution for today—and if he is calm and happy the moment they are out of your sight, that may seem like the right thing to do—it is not a good way to make a child feel that leaving Mom is safe and going with Dad is fun. In fact, a child who is physically forced is likely to remember his fear and frustration and anticipate those horrible feelings next time a visit is proposed. An older child may meet insistence that he go on a contact visit with passive resistance. A teenager will often refuse contact by locking himself in his room and refusing to appear for the intended handover or journey. Occasionally an older child or teenager who is ambivalent about both parents and the visit they have arranged for him will turn the tables by going with his father, as planned, and then refusing to return home at the end of a visit.

Problems at handover obviously affect (and are enormously distressing for) you both. Don't try to sort them out in front of the child. If this is the first time it's come up and you haven't planned how to cope, it may be best not to go on trying to force the issue this time but to arrange to talk to your ex about it later. If you are not on direct telephoning terms, you'll need to enlist whoever has helped you in mediation or specifically in making visitation arrangements. It is urgent. If you allow visits to go on starting with hysterical distress, or if you allow the distress to cancel the visits, the relationship between father and child can only get worse.

Secret Fears

Sometimes a child has a reason for refusing contact, which she is unwilling or unable to tell you about. Reasons sometimes include previous physical, sexual, or emotional abuse or the child having felt frighteningly unsafe during earlier contact.

No child should be compelled into contact that frightens her or makes her anxious and uneasy. If this seems to be the case, an expert assessment of each family member in relation to the others needs to be carried out so as to establish not only the facts but also the feelings of all concerned. Does the other parent press for regular visits with the child because he loves and misses her, or is his motive concerned with keeping control over you? Does the child really hate his father as he says, or does he think you will be pleased if he says that? Talk to a lawyer or to a social worker about assessment and the possibility of a subsequent application to the court for an order restricting contact.

Adult woman looking back to when she was eleven
"My little sister and I had to spend three weeks of the summer vacation with our father. He never actually did anything wrong, but I was always terrified that he would. Like if I forgot something (there was a gate I always forgot to shut), he'd say, 'What shall I do? Shall I spank you?' Or when I came out of the bath (the bathroom was downstairs) in pajamas, he'd say, 'There's my pretty girl; come and give a lonely man a big cuddle.' I know it sounds harmless but it wasn't. But how could I have explained to my mom?"

Separation Anxiety

The most common reason for serious problems over contact is separation anxiety, which is global rather than specific and is not due to any inappropriate behavior by the parent. Most babies and toddlers are liable to get anxious when they are parted from the parent they are most attached to. Contact with the nonresident parent (usually Dad) almost always means leaving Mom and home. Crying, clinging, and tantrums are normal reactions to separation, from late in the first year until around four years old, but the intensity and timing vary widely from child to child. Some children will go on getting anxious about leaving you (or having you leave them) all through the elementary school years. That's what those Sunday-night blues or Monday-morning tummy aches are about.

> **Mother of boy, aged six**
> "For a while he got so upset about school, and I got so upset at having to leave him crying in his classroom, that I wondered if I should let him have a break at home with me. But children do have to go to school, don't they? It seemed better that he should face that . . . By Thanksgiving he only cried on Monday mornings, and by the next term he didn't cry at all!"

In intact families and ordinary circumstances, separation anxiety becomes less frequent and less intense as the child grows up. In the meantime, you can do a lot to ease it by being understanding and sympathetic about your child's anxious feelings while also being firm and clear that what is being asked of him is safe and what he should do.

SOME CHILDREN'S SEPARATION ANXIETY doesn't just go away and stay away, though, but lasts for months or years and is so severe that it gets in the way of all the child's normal activities, developing into what many health professionals call separation anxiety disorder. Developmentally normal separation anxiety shares many signs and symptoms with separation anxiety disorder, but they differ in the intensity of your child's fears and how little it takes to set them off. If your child is moving into separation anxiety disorder, being left alone in bed while you go downstairs may cause panic, and just the thought of leaving the house without you may be enough to upset her.

Separation anxiety is about a child feeling unsafe. In the very early years your child's attachment to you means that she feels unsafe whenever you aren't there or available to her if she needs you (see chapter 2). Later on, and if the more extreme separation anxiety disorder develops, it will be because something has thrown the child off-balance, made her feel threatened and unable to cope or to manage herself and her world, and therefore to feel extra-dependent on you to do it for her.

Many separate life events can play a part in increasing normal separation anxiety or tipping a susceptible child toward separation anxiety disorder. But other than the death of a parent, nothing is more likely to bring those separate events together than parental separation.

When you separate, your child may face:

- Loss of a parent.
- Loss of other love objects, such as caregivers or pets.
- Changes in her environment, such as a new house, school, or day care.
- The stress associated with all the above changes.
- Your anxiety and distress, which she will sense and which will feed her own.

If your child's separation anxiety is within ordinary limits except that it is inappropriate for his age, there is a lot you can do to help him to feel safer, especially if the other parent will play his part:

- Practice separation. Make visits very brief at first, then gradually extend them as the child becomes more positive (or less anxious) about leaving you to go with Dad.

- For babies and toddlers, schedule visits for times of day when the child is at his most calm and cheerful—often in the second half of the afternoon, after lunch and a nap.
- Have a special good-bye ritual that you use whenever the child is separated from you and that he will therefore find reassuring when he leaves you to go with the other parent. Don't prolong the departure, though. Keep it as brief as a hug, a kiss on the nose, and a few words such as "Love you. See you soon. Have fun."
- Try to have the separation take place in familiar surroundings. If the visit cannot start from home without raising your stress level intolerably, try making the handover in another neutral, familiar place such as a grandparent's home.
- When a small child leaves, make sure he takes a familiar and beloved toy or cuddly with him (but make sure the other parent realizes it is important and doesn't let it get lost during the outing).
- However upset the child is, try not to give in and let him stay at home with you after all. He needs to know that you and the other parent are both confident that he will be OK and have a good time without you.

Separation Anxiety Disorder

The above tips may do something to help the child with separation anxiety disorder and will certainly do no harm. But it is important to realize how much more serious separation anxiety disorder is than separation anxiety.

In separation anxiety disorder, your child will feel constantly worried—every hour of every day—in case something happens that might lead to him being separated from you and acutely fearful when something does. The fear that overwhelms him will probably be one or more of the following:

- Fear that if he goes away something terrible will happen to someone he loves, most commonly that terrible harm (an accident, an illness, a murder, insanity) will come to you while he is gone. When children cannot leave home to go to school, it is not entirely school they fear but what may happen to a parent in their absence.

> **Grandmother recalls herself, aged seven**
> "Every day, coming home on the bus, I'd see myself going in by the kitchen door and Mommy being there but being quite crazy, so she didn't recognize me."

- Worry that once he is separated from you, something—such as getting lost or being kidnapped—will happen to make the separation permanent.
- Nightmares about being taken away from you or about losing you in a forest or watching you vanish into the sea.

Because of these fears, a child with separation anxiety disorder may:

- Refuse to go anywhere without you, which means that he not only refuses planned contact with the other parent but also school and playdates with friends.
- Be extremely reluctant to be left alone in bed and terrified to go to sleep.
- Suffer from a range of psychosomatic complaints such as headaches and tummy aches.
- Prefer to be within touch or sight of you all the time so that if he is small he may literally cling on to you as you move around and if he is older he may shadow you from room to room, even waiting for you outside the bathroom like a toddler.

What You Can Do to Help the Child with Separation Anxiety Disorder

Anything you can do to make your child feel safer in herself, her life, her home, and her relationships can help. Even if you cannot completely solve the problem, your understanding and sympathy can only make things better.

- Find out all you can about separation anxiety disorder and what your child is suffering so that it is clear to her that you understand. Older children in particular recognize that their fears are fantastical and are afraid of not being taken seriously.
- Listen carefully to anything your child will tell you about her feelings. Encourage her to talk; there's nothing to be gained by trying not to think about it.
- Remind the child—gently—that despite all that angst, he or she survived the last separation and all the separations before it.
- Anticipate times that are likely to cause separation difficulty and try different ways of helping. If your child finds it easier to separate from you at home than at the school bus, get a friend to take her instead of you and get your ex to start contact visits from the friend's home.
- Provide as consistent a daily pattern at home as you can. Don't underestimate the importance of predictability for children with separation anxiety problems. If the contact arrangements are going to change or a visitor is coming to stay, discuss it with your child ahead of time. During the months when anxiety is acute, try not to accept work or social commitments for yourself at such short notice that the child unexpectedly finds that you are not at home.
- Be careful not to let your child's anxiety buy endless indulgence. She needs your sympathy but she needs behavioral boundaries, too, or her life is likely to become more and more restricted. Let your child know that although you understand her feelings about going to bed, to school, or on parental visits, she does have to go, and remind her how well she managed last time.
- Offering the child choices or elements of control in an activity or an interaction with an adult may help him or her to feel safer and more comfortable. If she has to go to her Saturday soccer, ask her how she would prefer to manage the journey and being there without you.

Your own patience and know-how can certainly help your child with separation anxiety disorder, but it may not be enough, especially in a family breakdown situation. Some children with separation anxiety disorder need professional intervention. Assessments carried out for the court or by expert witnesses will establish whether your child is one of these.

> **Girl, aged ten**
>
> "You know what makes a really big, huge difference? Knowing that Mom will be there to meet me when school or something else I have to do without her finishes. Just thinking about her waiting at the gate really helps. I know it's babyish being met, but she says, 'Better met than absent!'"

WILLING CHILD AND RELUCTANT PARENT

Almost all the parents who abandon contact with their children are fathers. Not only are there very many fewer nonresident mothers, but research statistics from many countries show that they are very much more likely to stay in touch with their children year after year and through thick and thin.

If a nonresident father doesn't want to see his child, or even have indirect contact with her, there is nothing the mother can do to make him. He is legally obliged to pay child support, but that's only money; it has nothing to do with emotional support or contact. It seems ironic that a mother is legally obliged to encourage even the most reluctant children to have contact with their willing father, but she has no legal support for keeping willing children in touch with a nonresident father who doesn't want them.

Many of the men who have no contact with their children had no more than passing contact with the mothers. If the two parents never lived together and the father saw the baby only a few times (or not at all), his vanishing act will not affect the child as badly as being deserted by a father who is known and loved. Don't assume, though, that a child you have brought up on your own will not want to know who his father is and why he didn't

184 WHEN PARENTS PART

stick around. Some mothers who marry someone who is not the father within a year or two of a child's birth wonder if it is necessary for him to know that his stepfather (who may become his adoptive father) is not his biological father. All the evidence indicates that a child should know the truth as soon as you judge him old enough, not only because we all need to know our backgrounds and where we came from but also because deception and lies within families almost always come out. If your child eventually discovers (perhaps because you and his stepfather eventually separate) that the man he has always called Daddy is not his natural father, he will feel that the whole of his childhood has been thrown into uncertainty and everything he knew or felt about his family was false.

Boy, now aged sixteen
"I haven't seen my dad since I was thirteen. For the longest time—like years—I went on being really excited when he turned up and completely believing of his excuses when he didn't. My mom was really good about that. But then there was a birthday when he didn't even send a card, and then another birthday, and then I sort of realized he'd gone. I wish I knew where he's gone, though, because I really need to ask him what I did to make him just not care about me."

The next-largest group of vanishing fathers consists of men whose parenting after separation or divorce is not mutual or even polite but broken and eventually nonexistent. These are often men who get so worn down by the difficulties of negotiating with their exes and keeping to visitation schedules with their children that they give up. Regular weekends gradually become irregular invitations, and daytime or holiday visits become unpredictable and rare. Eventually they just don't happen anymore. For a while—and especially if mothers keep pressing for contact—the easier kinds, such as phone calls and texts, may carry on. But a vicious circle operates such that as contact dwindles it becomes more effortful. What do you say in a quick text to a fourteen-year-old if you haven't spoken to him or her in six months?

The last group of vanishing fathers—and thankfully the

smallest—consists of men who, however agonizing the decision, do just decide to go. Some of them leave the state or the country and make a new kid-free start. Some of them have girlfriends who wouldn't want anything to do with a child from an earlier relationship. Some of them hope that if they stop seeing you and the children, they can stop paying child support. Not all of these vanishing fathers jump out of their children's lives entirely of their own accord, though. Some of them are worn down by ceaseless criticism and disapproval, low-level alienation perhaps, from their exes. A few are more or less pushed out by their children's mothers and either do not realize that they can seek help with visitation from the court or cannot face—or afford—a continuing struggle (see chapter 6).

However it comes about, the loss to children whose parents vanish is almost worse than actual bereavement. Unless he kills himself, a father does not die because he wants to leave, and even children, guilt-prone though they are, cannot believe that it's their fault he had a heart attack or crashed his car. But if a father just leaves, it is obviously because he chooses to, and the fact that he made that choice tells his child that she is somehow to blame: she wasn't clever enough or good enough; she wasn't lovable enough or she didn't tell her father she loved him often enough. Grief and guilt is a toxic combination, and most mothers really struggle to find an alternative set of explanations that make sense but are less painful for the heartbroken child. When she asks, "Why doesn't Daddy come and see me or call me anymore?," there isn't an answer that won't hurt. If it's clear that your ex really has dumped the child, you probably can't do better than explain that when things have gone very wrong for people, they sometimes feel that they have to get themselves out of it however they can and without thinking about how much other people will be hurt. You might want to say that behaving that way isn't admirable but certainly doesn't suggest that the child has done anything wrong. If you think your child is old enough to want to understand a little more, you might want to add that the only two people who were responsible for things going wrong and breaking up the family were her father and yourself and that you apologize for both of you for not having managed to stay together or to separate better.

Being in contact with both parents gives children a sense of their own identity. When one parent doesn't wish to be involved in the child's life, knowing *about* him is better than nothing. Try to make it clear to the child that you are able to talk about his father without getting too distressed, and make sure that your child has photos of himself with his father. If you can manage to remain on friendly terms with your absent ex's extended family, contact with his paternal grandparents may help, too.

One day your child may decide to try and trace their other parent, as many adopted children do. Just as it's tough for adoptive parents to see a child going all out to find someone who's had no contact with her for eighteen years during which they have been her loving and caring parents, so watching your beloved child trying to trace a vanished dad who walked out on her leaving you to be mother and father in one can leave you seething with sorrow and resentment. Try to work through all those bad feelings and come up feeling good about yourself, though, because if your child finds her dad, she may get rejected all over again and then she will need your support even more.

PART III

What Works and What Does Not

9

More Issues Parents Raise

P arents who separate often have to face practical and emotional problems that none of their advisers had mentioned and thus make decisions that they hadn't thought about in advance. Some of them have shared the issues that were most important to their children and the solutions they eventually reached.

HOLIDAYS

The routines and rhythms of life as a family with children are punctuated by special occasions. All families quickly accumulate their own ceremonies and ways of celebrating them, which children expect and look forward to. It's not only the big, personally important days like birthdays or public holidays such as Christmas, New Year's Day, and Thanksgiving that are important. There are also religious holidays such as Eid and Yom Kippur that matter very much to particular groups of families, and a few that are part of daily life for some, such as Shabbat for observant Jews. And along with all of those there are many lower-key "special days," which your family might or might not have chosen to celebrate, such as Valentine's Day, Mother's Day, and Halloween.

Just as important as many of those—if not more so—are occasions that individual families invent and celebrate for themselves, like a special dinner to mark the last night of each school semester. Any of these—and many others—might have become part of the fabric of your children's family lives, and if family life has disintegrated, what is to become of them? Birthdays still happen, of course, but they may not feel celebratory with one parent (and a sad one at that) taking part instead of two. Christmas dominates schools and shopping malls for months, but the inescapable carols make separated adults and older children think nostalgically about last year and younger children sober at their sad faces. And what about the family's own fun breaks? Will the Sunday lunch with grandparents and the Friday movie night carry on now that the routines of daily life that they used to break up are no longer in place? Everybody loses so much when a family breaks down that losing special days and holidays may sound trivial. It doesn't feel trivial to children, though. Losing those eagerly anticipated punctuation marks in ordinary life that they used to plan for will leave holes in children's lives, and the desperate difficulty of finding ways to replace or continue them is something that many parents struggle with.

The best way to rescue the special days that matter most to your family from the doldrums of divorce is to be proactive in changing what you celebrate and exactly how. The actions that are open to you crucially depend on circumstances, of course, and on how much energy and head space you can muster. If you separated in April and it's now October, you may not be able to bear even to think about Christmas. But even if you don't think about it, Christmas will come and cannot be ignored. You all have to get through it somehow, and how you do that will really matter to any child who is old enough to remember last year.

Younger married sister

"Lily's only nine months, so Christmas at home seems a bit silly. She isn't going to open a stocking or eat turkey. So we'd probably have gone to Mom and Dad, but this way we can all be together and it'll be great."

The circumstance that matters most is your relationship with each other as parents—specifically, whether you can ever be in the same place at the same time so that the children can have you both on occasions that are really important to them. If sharing space is a step too far, can your children at least have the benefit of your shared thinking about them—including what one wants for his birthday or what another plans to put on a Christmas list for Santa? Even if the answer to both questions is a less polite version of no, you can still be proactive, but it will be a great deal easier if the answer is yes. The following ways forward are highly recommended:

> **Paternal grandmother of boy, aged two, and two girls, aged four and six**
> "We'll not go; that's for sure. Well, we won't, will we? I mean, I wouldn't go to her home after the way she's treated Jake . . . but I do miss those little monsters, and if he'll be there—well, maybe we could . . . "

> **Paternal great-aunt**
> "Our son is grown up and he and his family are in New Zealand. It's years since we had a proper house full of children at Christmas."

- Instead of trying to make the big holidays such as Christmas or Thanksgiving just as they have always been but with only one parent, turn outward and put the emphasis on making it an extended family day; his family as well as yours, if any relations live near enough. If there are any who live within reach but have not been on speaking terms with you since the separation, this is the kind of initiative that often breaks down those barriers. Even if people are scattered, this idea can work if somebody in the family has the will to adopt it. There may be one person with a large home who will host a family get-together or someone who will rent a cottage for the family to use during winter break. Once you float the idea, you may be surprised by how many people there are who would welcome it and be prepared to travel for it, not just for your and the children's sakes but for their own as well.

- Making the "family" in family celebration into "extended family" means, of course, that the other parent is welcome to come and take part, and the fact that people from his side of the family are invited should make it easier for him to accept. Even if he refuses to take part in the planning, he'll be kept fully informed of the plans, and if in the end he doesn't come, his absence will be far less noticeable in a crowd gathered in a different place than it would have been at home. It is not that his children won't miss their daddy, of course; he's irreplaceable. But because their Christmas or Thanksgiving doesn't rely on you and him but on you and other family members, his absence is less likely to mean that it all falls apart.

- Opening up the tight little world of the nuclear family can work even if you have no actual extended family to open up to. Among your close friends with children in the same age groups as yours, it's very likely that there are one or two who are in a similar situation to yours and would welcome pooling support and resources on some occasions. And if you know someone who is completely on her own, an invitation to Christmas dinner at your home might transform the holiday not only for her but also for you and the children, because entertaining guests makes everything different.

If one of these ideas works for you one year, it could be the pattern for years to come, cementing relationships with your children's wider family or your community, enlarging your friendship group, and ensuring that your children never have to eat two Christmas or Thanksgiving dinners.

Birthdays really matter to children and many report being hurt or offended by birthday arrangements that were made over their heads to suit separated parents. The problem is that children's birthdays are important to parents, too, so there is often competition between mother and father over who a child will be with for the big day. Sometimes parents insist that the two of them should have the birthday child on alternate years. Sometimes the arrangement is that she will celebrate her birthday in whichever household she happens to be.

If the two of you are ever going to get together to make an occasion for your children, birthdays are excellent occasions to make the effort. Some separated parents whose children are school age or older swear by a birthday dinner in a restaurant for the child and his best friend(s) because as well as being a big treat for the birthday child, being in public and in a formal setting helps parents to be polite to each other.

There are other ways for your child to have both of you involved in a birthday that don't mean you have to set eyes on each other. In intact families, when a child's actual birthday falls on a school day, it is often split from birthday celebrations, which need to take place on the weekend. That same idea can work for separated parents, with the parent the child mostly lives with doing the actual birthday and the other parent planning a birthday trip or treat for the next visit. A birthday *party* will need to be held close to home, school, and guests and either on a weekend or during the holidays, so if a child normally goes to her father every weekend and the birthday falls during school time, this is one of the occasions when regular contact arrangements need you to be friendly and flexible (see pp. 108–13).

> **Mother of girl, aged eight, and boy, aged six**
>
> "Last Christmas was just after we split up and we spent it here, sort of trying to copy the year before. It was horrible. One of the worst days of the whole separation. This year had to be different. We don't have family in this country, and although friends invited us, my daughter wanted to be at home for Christmas Day, so we thought instead of having an empty place at table we'll fill it up. We invited an elderly neighbor who has a little dog the children simply loved and a young woman who's on her own with a baby (the children liked the baby, too, but not as much as the dog). She's now my precious babysitter. It wasn't just a really good day; it was also a day that made me realize I could still do nice and worthwhile things with and for the children on my own."

Celebrations such as Halloween are actually more fun for children when more people are involved, and you don't always have to be the one who plays hostess. There may be a get-together that another parent at your child's school or day care is helping with and to which you and yours would be welcome. Or there may be a community gathering for New Year's that offers fun for all ages. The idea is that doing *something* special keeps the occasion fun for your children, but that not doing the same as you used to do makes it easier for you.

> **Young man, aged twenty**
> "The birthday thing made me furious all through my teens. How dare they say I'd got to stay with Mom for it this year 'because it's her turn'? My birthday, not anybody else's turn."

When it comes to your previous family's private celebratory traditions, you don't have to keep up every single one. There are probably some that your children will not notice or miss. But some formerly private traditions—maybe the barbecue that celebrates the last night of the school year—also lend themselves to being shared with other families. Children often know surprisingly little about one another's home circumstances, but there's a good chance that some of your children's friends have parents in a similar position to theirs. Discovering that, and spending time together as two still-surviving families, may be helpful to all the children and to you adults as well.

Summer Vacations

Parenting agreements, whether made by the court, worked out with mediators, or agreed to privately by fathers and mothers, often include the right for the nonresident parent to take the children on a summer vacation. All the considerations that apply to overnight or weekend contact with the other parent also apply to going away on vacation (see pp. 152–70) However, vacations do provoke particular difficulties, though many might have arisen even if your family had remained intact. These are family vacation problems rather than post-separation problems, but if one of you is going to cope with them alone, it's important to be aware of them.

- A teenage girl may much prefer the company of peers to parents and may not want to come. If she is made to come, she may sulk the whole time.
- A teenage boy may not be so devoted to his peers but may only look forward to a vacation that has planned goals and will very likely enjoy one only if it has physical activities built in.
- Elementary school aged children are probably the easiest to please, and the same kinds of vacation will often suit both girls and boys, but a single child is likely to be lonely and bored and extremely hard work for the parent who must also be playmate. If it's financially possible to arrange it, inviting a school friend along can work well.
- Most children are reluctant sightseers (so might not think there is much to do in cities), and many get very bored on long car journeys. Children under about eight seem almost incapable of being interested in anything they see out of the windows of a moving car, so if you want them to get anything out of going through those mountains or seeing those wild horses, you have to allow the time to keep stopping so they can get out.

Problems that are specific to nonresident fathers taking children on vacation are most likely to arise when you are taking a very young child or when you are taking several children of different genders and very mixed ages.

Whatever his age, if a child already looks forward to and enjoys staying overnight with you, there is every reason to suppose that you can successfully go on vacation together. But if a child is under four—especially if he is a baby or toddler—and not yet accustomed to staying with you away from mother and home, a vacation may not be the best way for either of you to start. Not only will the child be away from his mom, he will also be staying in novel surroundings—whether hotel, B and B, rented apartment, camper, or tent—which he may find strange and bewildering, eating different food, and living without his accustomed routine. You will therefore be caring for him on your own for the first time in circumstances that are likely to make him unusually needy or demanding. Start with a brief trial run such as a holiday weekend, and try for a homelike environment such as a farm guesthouse.

If a child is approaching seven and seems ready to spend a real vacation with you, keep the first one fairly brief—a week away from mother and home is plenty long enough—and stay within easy traveling distance. Roughly 10 percent of this age group are liable to become overwhelmingly homesick, and if yours should be one of them, you need to be able to bring her home. Several fathers who have been through this warn that if you are on a package vacation in another country, flight restrictions may mean that you cannot cut the trip short. If a child is forced to go on with the vacation when she is desperate to go home, she won't remember the parts she enjoyed, such as the lovely beaches, the warm sea, and the best-ever ice cream; her recollection of the whole trip will be dominated by memories of her misery, and the next time you suggest a vacation, she probably will not want to come.

Girl, aged seven

"When I stayed in the sun too long and got sick, I told Dad I wanted my mom and I wanted to go home. He was OK with it and went to ask about flights, but when he came back and said we couldn't go till the end of the week, I got really upset. I think it was knowing we couldn't that was the bad part."

- If she is accustomed to coming to stay with you at the same time as older siblings, make sure that at least one of them is included in the vacation.
- Agree with your ex that the child will be allowed—and helped—to contact her while she is away if she wants to. A brief daily good-night phone or video call may really help her; on the other hand it may actually provoke homesickness. Make sure

that any calls she makes are for her benefit rather than for her mother's.

- If there is only one child involved in a vacation and she or he is older—ten or over, perhaps—it should be possible to think of a trip that is tailored to him or her and affordable and at least tolerable to you. Your fourteen-year-old daughter might always have longed to go to LA, for example, while a thirteen-year-old son wants to cycle or climb, and a nine-year-old only wants to play on the beach. You may be willing, even eager, to do any of those things, but you can do them only one at a time, so if you are taking several children on vacation, you will have to find a compromise destination that offers at least something each child will enjoy. If you were one of two adults, you could divide the activities between you, taking turns so that each child could do the things he or she liked most. But as a single parent on vacation with two or three children, you are up against a real difficulty, which is that everybody has to do the same things at the same time, whether they like it or not. And sometimes they won't.

- Some separated fathers turn to their own parents, either to join in vacations with the children or, if they have plenty of space and enough for children to do, to provide them. If money is not a problem, sharing rented vacation accommodations with grandparents can work well for everybody, giving all three generations a chance to live together for a few days.

- Some parents recommend packages that offer exciting children's clubs and so many supervised activities—from water sports to disco dancing—that an older child will find something to enjoy at any moment of the day. Family-friendly resorts (there are hundreds of them advertising on the Internet) pride themselves on this. However, shy children may find it difficult to join in. And these vacations are far from cheap.

- If you are going it alone, beaches and water—the ocean or perhaps a lake—are probably your best bet, provided you go somewhere the sun is likely to shine, so that if your teenage daughter is not in the mood for bathing in cold water (even in a wet suit) she can lie about and read instead. Do allow for the fact that children under about twelve cannot safely be permitted in the water for a single minute without an adult, even if they are strong swimmers (probably in a swimming pool), nor be trusted to stay out of it until you get back from taking their smaller sibling to the bathroom.

Meeting the demands of everyone's safety and enjoyment makes a beach a highly stressful place for a single parent. If a small child wants to make sand castles and a bigger one wants to swim, one adult isn't enough unless you also have a teenager who will help supervise younger ones.

- Most people agree that it's easier for two adults to supervise six children (and stay sane) than for one adult to supervise two or three, so you might consider sharing your vacation with another single-parent family.

PRESSURES TOWARD INDEPENDENCE FROM ADULTS

As if coping with no longer being a spouse was not difficult enough, the practicalities of daily life as a suddenly single parent can take you unawares and need a lot of organizing. Even if the children's care has always fallen mostly to you, their father probably played a far bigger part than was obvious until he was gone. Because he was in the house, you could leave one child at home while you picked up or did something with another when the need arose, or leave them all playing while you made an efficiency trip to the supermarket, or get him to pick up the teenager from her party while you did the baby's late-evening feeding. Now that there isn't a second adult in the house, you will often need to be in two places at once.

Why is this any different for recently separated families than for families that have had a single parent for years—or perhaps from the beginning? Parents say that it's different because single parenting after separation is a new situation and change of lifestyle that contradicts the experience and expectations of both mother and children. It raises many questions they haven't needed to address before, many of them to do with whether or not children are old enough to be unsupervised.

> **Father of boy, aged nine, and girl, aged eleven**
> "I don't know how she'll manage. I drive a taxi and I've always been able to take a break to meet the kids from the bus or pick my daughter up from school clubs and stuff. My wife—I should say my ex-wife—doesn't get home until six, so I don't know what she'll do."

Being at Home Alone

When mothers and fathers both have jobs outside their homes, they often fill any gaps between their working hours and children's school hours between them. The most common is that gap between the end of the school day and the end of the work-and-travel day, but gaps between leaving times in the morning are also commonplace, often with mother leaving early (so as to get home early) and father seeing children off to school before leaving himself. When father moves out, or mother and children

---

PARENTS' VIEWS OF AGES FOR CHILDREN TO BE UNSUPERVISED

Average ages given by parents for:

  Walking to school alone: ten years
  Staying home alone for a few hours: thirteen years
      (though some said eight; some said eighteen)
  Minimum age to take a train alone: thirteen years
  Youngest age for an unaccompanied plane journey: fourteen years
  Youngest age to be left alone at home overnight: fifteen years
  Youngest age at which it is appropriate for a child to be left at home for
      a weekend: seventeen years

Source: Thompson 2011

GUIDELINE AGES FOR LEAVING CHILDREN HOME ALONE

Below are general guidelines for parents who are considering the age range for leaving a child home alone.

Seven and under: Should not be left alone for any period of time. This may include leaving children unattended in cars, playgrounds, and backyards. The determining consideration would be the dangers in the environment and the ability of the caretaker to intervene.

Eight to ten years: Should not be left alone for more than one and a half hours and only during daylight and early evening hours.

Eleven to twelve years: May be left alone for up to three hours but not late at night or in circumstances requiring inappropriate responsibility.

Thirteen to fifteen years: May be left unsupervised, but not overnight.

Sixteen to seventeen years: May be left unsupervised (in some cases, for up to two consecutive overnight periods).

Source: U.S. Department of Health and Human Services, Administration for Children and Families, Child Welfare Information Gateway, www.childwelfare.gov

live somewhere else without him, there's only half the adult gap-filling power.

All these gaps raise the same question: Is this particular child old enough to cope on his own? Will he be all right letting himself into an empty house and being there alone for a couple of hours? Or, will my daughter cope with being left on her own at breakfast time and getting herself off to school (locking the front door behind her)?

- Many parents look in vain for clear legal regulation or even for guidance that applies across states. Only three states currently have laws regarding a minimum age for leaving a child home alone. Illinois law requires children to be fourteen years old before being left; in Oregon, children must be ten years old; while in Maryland, the minimum age is eight.

- The child protection laws of most states classify "failing to provide adequate supervision of a child" as child neglect, but they provide little detail on what is considered "adequate supervision." Charges of neglect may result from any combination of factors that puts the child at risk of harm, including the child's age, mental ability, physical condition, the length of the parent's absence, or the home environment.

- Whatever a child's age (if he is under sixteen), you can be charged with willful neglect if you leave him "in a manner likely to cause unnecessary suffering or injury to health"; otherwise it is up to you—and him.

- Fifteen million children from intact families do come back from school to empty houses and occupy themselves until a parent comes home. However, it may be somewhat more of a challenge for children from single-parent homes, such as your eleven- or twelve-year-old, not only because he isn't used to it but also because it emphasizes the loneliness that he is probably already feeling because of the other parent's absence. In fact, an important consideration in this and all other "home alone" situations is what the child feels about it. A big study of latchkey children in the United States found that a sadly high percentage of them dreaded the time spent alone in the house, and many were anxious, even frightened, especially in winter when they returned to a house in darkness.

- It's very unlikely that an elementary school child will cope safely and comfortably with regularly coming home to an empty house. If you are seriously considering this for an eight- or nine-year-old, ask yourself whether you are sure he can remember to take the door key with him, remember where he has put it, and, above all, easily persuade it to turn. Once in the house, does he know where all the light switches are? Can he get himself a snack? And, above all, can he use a phone? He needs to be able to call you to report that he's safely home and to hear your voice; he needs to be able to phone a friendly adult

**One of a pair of twin boys,
then aged nine**
"The worst was the time I locked Joe
in the bathroom and then couldn't make
the catch-thing work. He got panicky, so
I got the stepladder out of the shed so
he could climb out of the window. Only
the window wasn't big enough, and he
got stuck. Would I have thought to call
911 or even the neighbor whose number
was written by the phone? Nope. It was
pure luck that she heard Joe yelling."

who is close by (and always in)
if he is worried about anything;
and he also needs to know that
he should dial 911 in any
emergency and that when the
person who answers asks him
what service he wants, she
means "What's up?" and he
should tell her. The harsh
truth, though, is that if there
really is an emergency—the
boiler catches fire, a gale blows
a window in, or there's a
burglar upstairs—he will be far too frightened to do anything
sensible. If your number is on speed dial, he might call you, but
you are really gambling on nothing untoward happening—
a reasonable bet, perhaps, if he will be alone for twenty
minutes; not so good if it will be two hours.

■ Two children together are less likely to be lonely and scared
but perhaps more likely to get themselves into trouble, either
because they quarrel or because a fun game goes haywire.

A ten- and a thirteen-year-old may be all right on their own
for an hour or so, but even the thirteen-year-old should not be
expected to look after a much younger sibling (see pp. 204–6).
Some parents find better solutions to the gap between hours
of adult work and children's school:

■ According to the After-School Alliance, 8.4 million children
already attend after-school programs designed for exactly
this, or there may be after-school activities that fill the gap
while fulfilling a different purpose, such as teaching drama
or gymnastics or sports. Be wary of programs held on school
premises, though; in many smaller schools they rely on
the enthusiastic presence of one teacher and are therefore

liable to sudden cancellation if she is away. And if you have children at more than one school, matching up their after-school programs may be a nightmare.

- If you have good links in the community, you may be able to find a much older student—a seventeen-year-old, perhaps—who has tests coming up and a load of homework but is also keen to earn money and would therefore be pleased to walk your children home and stay with them until you get there.

- In some towns there may be a licensed family day care provider who has opted to concentrate on before- and after-school care and has space to include your children. Some teenagers feel demeaned by this suggestion, but many find a new friendship group in the caregiver's home and some go on dropping in for an after-school snack long after they really *are* old enough to be at home alone.

- If you are very fortunate, there may be a grandparent or other relative who lives locally, does not work full-time, and would like to help.

- The very best solution comes with so many "ifs" that it's rare, but if the children's father lives nearby, his work is flexible or freelance, and you and he are trying to be mutual parents, filling those gaps may be his major contribution to everyone's well-being.

The home-alone problem is not only about school, of course. If you are able to go on with whatever arrangements you used to make during school vacations before the family breakup, the continuity in their uncertain world will be especially welcome to your children. But if their father used to undertake much of their care during the school vacations and is not able or prepared to do so now, your separation may mean that you have to make new plans. Unfortunately, what you were able to afford as an intact couple may be completely out of reach now that you are separated; 33 percent of all families sent at least one child to a summer program in 2013, but the program was free for fewer than 15 percent of them, and the average cost to the rest was $250 per child per week.

Young Babysitters

The law says nothing about how old a person has to be before he or she can babysit, although twelve to thirteen years old is often given as a guideline. If you leave your child with anyone who is younger than sixteen, you, not the babysitter, remain legally responsible for the child's safety. So while under-sixteens can babysit, they cannot take legal responsibility for a child, and if something dangerous happens to him, you will be blamed (and no doubt blame yourself). So, as with leaving children at home alone, leaving them with an underage babysitter, even their own sibling, is a calculated risk. If there was a fire or a dangerous accident, a child became seriously ill, or an intruder broke in, there's only another child to cope.

> **Mother of two boys, aged eighteen months and ten years, and a girl, aged eight**
> "On my own with the baby 24/7 and the other two when they weren't at school, I just felt trapped. I couldn't move. Couldn't run to the store or have a coffee with my friend next door like I used to while my ex watched sports on TV. So I did used to get the boy to babysit until their father found out and said he'd tell the welfare lady. So now I'm stuck."

- Know the babysitter. If it's not your own older child but somebody else's, don't employ him or her until he or she is at least twelve and even then try to get some word-of-mouth recommendations.
- If the prospective babysitter is your own older child, will he take the responsibility seriously? Will the younger child or children do as he says? Does he know how to keep safe at home and whom to phone if he needs help?
- Don't take even this small risk with a baby. Even if she is asleep in her crib, she could throw up and choke or spike a

really high fever. She almost certainly won't, but she *could*, and if she did, a very young and inexperienced babysitter wouldn't know what to do. Parents are often advised to encourage young babysitters to take the American Red Cross babysitters' class, but possession of that certificate can give parents false confidence: knowing what to do is one thing; having the calm confidence to do it in an emergency is quite another.

- Don't take the risk with a toddler either; in inexperienced hands he could (and very likely would) put something small enough to choke on in his mouth, which the child in charge probably won't anticipate, or he could fall over something or down the stairs or off the chair he climbed onto. He may or may not bang his head hard enough to matter, but it takes experience to judge.
- If you leave a preschooler or kindergartener with a very young babysitter, keep the time you're away really short. Children in that age group can have all manner of accidents in the home, of course, but the chances of your child doing so in any single hour are low. You can probably get some chores done around the neighborhood or briefly visit a friend but not go out for the evening.

Many suddenly single mothers count on getting breaks when children go to stay with their father, on weekends or during the holidays. If you have a baby or toddler who cannot yet go away happily overnight, try not to let your need for freedom override her need to stay securely with you. Some mothers in this situation have managed to set up a single-parent babysitting swap scheme. The usual scheme by which couples take turns going out while one parent of another pair babysits their children can work only for couples, but single mothers can take turns going out

Mother of two girls, aged one and three
"Everyone knows I'm pretty stuck right now, so they've been really good about coming to mine. We had a friend's baby shower here and several birthdays."

while another mother and her children babysit for her. Whether they spend the night or are woken to go home when the mother comes in, both the host children and the babysitting children often enjoy these necessarily sociable evenings. Other mothers, especially those whose very young children don't settle well in a strange house even if Mom is there, resign themselves to going out only when a grandparent or girlfriend can babysit for them. In the meantime, they break up the feeling of being isolated with children by inviting friends over.

Traveling

Transporting children back and forth between their mother's home and their father's is a major issue in some separated families, and the farther apart parents live (and the scarcer their income), the bigger the problem. Parenting plans sometimes specify the way in which travel should be shared between the parents—often with each being responsible for 50 percent of the time and money involved—but such arrangements are not always honored, especially if there are ongoing tussles about access.

Traveling by Car

If the two homes are only just outside walking or cycling range, driving children between them is usually the quickest and the cheapest; it may even be the only means of transport, since small towns and country areas often have no buses that are convenient. Parents who both have cars and are cooperating to make visits as comfortable as possible often arrange to do one return journey each.

If the two homes are much farther apart, driving may take longer and gas may cost more than public transport. The car may still score for convenience, though. Some parents share time and expense by each driving half the distance, meeting, and transferring the children from one car to the other at an agreed-upon location.

Public Transportation

If a child or children can travel alone on public transportation from one parent's home to the other, parents save both their time and the cost of fares for the accompanying adult. Many parents ask how old a child needs to be before such travel is legal and safe.

BUSES

Most bus companies say that a child must be at least eight years old before she can travel alone. Some companies make provisions for unaccompanied eight- to fourteen-year-olds. The age at which a teenage sibling counts as an accompanying adult varies. Get information from the bus company that provides the service you want to use. If you don't know which that is, the American Intercity Bus Riders Association (AIBRA) gives national information.

An eight- or nine-year-old who is used to going to school by bus with other children may feel all right about a short, direct journey on her own as long as she is put on the bus by one adult at the beginning and met at the other end. However, if the journey is not brief enough to be comfortable for her on her own, it may be little more trouble and not overly expensive for one parent to go with her and the other to bring her back. In the course of those accompanied trips, she will learn the route and its landmarks so that she becomes more confident about doing the trip alone.

COACHES

Some coach companies, notably Greyhound at the time of writing, do not allow children under fourteen to travel without someone who is over sixteen and have strict regulations about the length of journey a child may undertake. That is unfortunate, because for longer journeys buses can be much easier for children to manage on their own than trains. Once installed on the right bus, the child has no decisions or choices to make; he simply stays put until the bus reaches its terminus, where he must be met.

Acceptance of the accompanying person being sixteen years old (rather than a full adult) is helpful to quite a lot of families in which several children, including a sixteen-year-old, travel to see the other parent.

TRAINS

The Amtrak network and its subsidiaries have very strict rules concerning child travelers. It has recently increased the minimum age at which an unaccompanied child may travel from twelve to thirteen years old. Anyone twelve years or younger must be accompanied by someone eighteen or over. Children may not travel on overnight trains or those arriving late in the evening. Only direct travel between two staffed stations is permitted, and there are ID checks for the adult dispatching and meeting the child.

Whether your child is ready to take a train on her own depends not only on her age, temperament, and good sense, but also the line she will be traveling on. Trains that get very full can be daunting and difficult to manage, especially as commuting adults seldom treat children as equal human beings.

If a child needs to leave a train at an intermediate station rather than the terminus, she may have a problem with knowing when she has arrived, especially if it is dark. Savvy parents provide children with a list of stations where the train will stop and the time it's due at their destination. Unfortunately, on any day but most especially on Sunday, a child may be faced with unscheduled timetable

> **Boy, aged ten**
>
> "I wanted to go by train 'cause that way I could go to my dad's every weekend, not just every other if Mom had to drive me. But the first time it got totally packed, and a man said I should give up my seat to a grown-up—'Haven't you any manners?' he said—and my bag was under the table and I got pushed away, so I thought I wouldn't be able to get it. I did, but it wasn't fun."

changes. So an hour on a quiet country route may be fine, but a journey that takes her through a big junction may become unmanageably complicated.

PLANES

If the nonresident parent moves to a different country, or even to a different state, a child's visits may depend on traveling by air. It costs a great deal of money to have an adult fly with a child, so you will probably want yours to fly alone as soon as possible. When that might be depends not only on the child's age and temperament but also on the kind of journey she has to make. An hour-long flight from one small airport directly to another may be comparatively easy. It will not be far from security, where you have to leave her, to the plane, and once she gets there all she has to do is to sit (reasonably) still until she gets off along with everyone else and sees the other parent waiting for her.

A long flight, and especially an international flight, is a very different matter. Navigating a seething airport is difficult enough for adults, terrifying for most children. You will have to rely on the airline staff employed to look after unaccompanied children. Because of increasing instances of child abduction in custody cases (as well as child trafficking), any immigration officer or airline official may ask you for a letter of "consent to travel" if your child is crossing national boundaries with one parent alone or with another adult.

In the United States, there are no clear regulatory guidelines from the Federal Aviation Administration with respect to unaccompanied children. Airlines are free to enforce any rules they want, and no two airlines will have exactly the same ones, so make sure you check with your airline before you buy your child's ticket. Most airlines allow children to fly alone, but the rules, restrictions, and charges imposed on unaccompanied children are different for each airline.

Airlines treat children traveling alone differently depending on their ages, and the special services they supply tend to be expensive. Most airlines have a minimum age for their unaccompanied-child service, typically five years, and a maximum age, typically twelve. Children younger than the minimum age will have to travel with an adult. If your child appears to be beyond the age limit set by the airline, you or your child may be asked to provide some kind of proof of the child's age, so make sure you have appropriate documentation with you at the airport.

If a child is older than an airline's maximum age for their unaccompanied-child program, that airline may allow the child to travel under their program's rules, but without using special services for unaccompanied children such as having an escort while at an airport or being allowed to board the aircraft early.

For unaccompanied children traveling under the airline's supervision, there may be additional restrictions and requirements. While the number and type of restrictions vary by airline, typical restrictions may include allowing unaccompanied children only on nonstop flights.

UNITED AIRLINES PROVIDES a typical program called the Young Travelers Club service, which is compulsory for children traveling alone between the ages of five and twelve, who are permitted only on nonstop flights. The same service is available to but optional for children between their twelfth and eighteenth birthdays. The service must be booked at the same time as the child's flight ticket. It is expensive.

When children fly alone, airlines (like parents!) are most concerned about complications such as transfers and stopovers, which is why many, like United, confine unaccompanied minors to nonstop flights. Airlines do vary, though, and if your child's proposed journey is more complicated, it is worth shopping around. Some will accept children on journeys that involve a night stop, airport transfer, or long daytime stopover provided arrangements have been made for an adult to meet and care for the child at the transfer points. The airline will require full contact details for this person as well as for the person who is to meet the child at the end of the journey, and there will be a substantial extra charge.

If your child is over twelve and eager to travel completely independently, allowing him to do so will save a lot of money. Do bear in mind, though, that if he is making an international flight, he will not only have to find his way through security and passport control and to the correct departure gate, he will also have to cope with any travel difficulty that comes up, as if he was an adult passenger. Is he confident enough in talking to adults that he would be able to cope if his baggage was lost, stolen, or damaged or his flight was delayed or even diverted to an airport where there will be nobody to meet him? If he is not met, will he manage to communicate with the parent who should be there, and with you? What will you advise him to do? Some airline staff are sympathetic to a young person on his own in such circumstances, but your child might get no extra help because staff are too busy with children whose parents have paid for their services and also, perhaps, too aware that you chose not to.

If this plane journey is to be an integral part of your child's life for the foreseeable future, it's worth doing everything you can to ensure that she doesn't have a nerve-wracking journey early on, for if she does she is likely to dread, even resist doing the same trip later on (see chapter 8). It will probably be wise—and well worth the expense—to make a trial run with the child before you commit him or her to flying alone. If the child is under twelve, you might accompany him the first time and use your airline's unaccompanied minor program thereafter. If he is over twelve, he may cope easily with a quick domestic flight, but for a more major trip it might be sensible to accept the option of the fly-alone service the first time and let him travel independently the next time, if he still feels confident.

BOARDING SCHOOLS

For a child whose parents are separating, there may be a period when "home" is both emotionally and practically chaotic, with short-notice swaps between the care of mother and father or even emergency arrangements for babysitters or people to do the school run. Most parents realize how damaging these levels of unpredictability and insecurity are for their children, but while most will look for ways to bring stability and security back into the home, some, especially the well-to-do, will consider sending the child away from home to find stability in boarding school.

Boarding schools have traditionally been seen to provide not only a highly privileged education but also stability and continuity for children whose parents—often in the military or diplomatic services—had to keep moving so that they would otherwise have had many changes of school. Now this stability and security is increasingly sought by parents such as the mother quoted above: people who are separating worse rather than better and can neither provide nor allow the other parent to provide a stable and secure home for their children. Boarding school in term-time and holiday visits to both parents may seem to be the answer, but is it?

Sometimes boarding school can indeed provide a safe place and saving routine for children whose home environments are

Mother of girl, aged thirteen
"I knew we couldn't go on like that. I meant to be home when she got back from school, but half the time I was in the middle of yet another agonizing discussion with her father and the other half I was in bed with J.

"I called in every favor I could from her school friends' mothers, but she hates being foisted on people at no notice. And then there was a weekend when J said, 'Come to Paris,' and I actually got in a temporary live-in nanny to take over. Yes, I'm ashamed. Yes, I did boarding school because I wanted her out of the way for my sake, but truly it did seem better for her, too."

chaotic. Boarding schools have changed, almost (but not quite) beyond recognition, so that some older children, especially teen-agers whose focus of attention has begun to move from parents to peers, beg to board. Many schools have day students as well as boarders, and some will ac-commodate children staying full-time, weekly, or even "on demand," providing all of them with a less institu-tionalized environment than used to be the case. Day stu-dents often say that because they go home each night and each weekend, they miss out on what their school has to offer. However, other chil-dren who go to boarding schools—especially younger ones and those who were sent rather than asked to go—are shocked by separa-tion and grieve for home and

> **Woman, now aged sixty**
> "My mother had left my father for another man when I was ten, and my father was beyond angry. My mother wanted me to live with her, and that's what I wanted, too, but although my father didn't want to look after me himself, he was determined that she shouldn't. So since she and my stepfather-to-be hadn't married yet, he did a sort of moral outrage thing and forbade my mom to have me to stay in their home. So I was packed off to boarding school. I didn't know what was happening at home. I didn't even really know where home was. I just felt abandoned."

parents. Even the youngest—tragic six- and seven-year-olds—eventually grow the survival shell that enables them to pretend they are flourishing: "I was a bit homesick," they say, "but it was good for me." They are wrong. It was not.

IF MODERN BOARDING SCHOOLS can be a good experience for some young people, they will not be for those who are sent away from home because separated parents want their own space and privacy or just cannot figure out what else to do with them. Such children arrive at school as exiles from the family life they knew before. They feel (and are) abandoned, and, very often, they feel that the dissolution of life as they knew it is their fault, and this

BOARDING SCHOOLS REDUCE PARENT-CHILD COMMUNICATION

"Missing out on the kind of contact with father we have been discussing is a great loss to a growing child, even if having any father around is becoming a luxury. Moreover, sending children away to boarding school can create a sense of the absence of both mother and father, unless the parents are extremely successful in keeping the emotional channels open with their child."

Source: Duffell 2000

banishment is their punishment. To make matters worse, the sentence may seem indefinite, because while other homesick children can look forward to returning to their familiar homes and secure families during the next spring break or vacation, these children do not know where they will be going or to whom they will return.

- The more muddled the situation is at home, the more important it is that your child should be there so she can see what's happening and, hopefully, see that on some basic level both her parents are OK and still love her.
- If you send her away, she will feel (rightly) that she has no control over what is left of her family life or over the decisions being made for her.
- Don't think that by sending your child away you protect her from seeing your unhappiness or the ugly arguments that are going on. If she cannot see what is really happening, she will imagine much worse.
- Children whose parents are separated are always at risk of feeling that they are somehow responsible: sending your child away will make her feel that she is being banished and punished.

LONG-DISTANCE PARENTING

In countless numbers of divorced families, long-distance parenting is the best that can be managed for one parent. We live in a mobile society. It is estimated that the average American family changes residence every five years, and many families move even more frequently. Even for intact families, relocating can be highly problematic, especially for children, but it is far worse when parents are separated, because one parent becomes a long-distance mom or dad, and that is one of the most difficult challenges facing divorced parents and their children.

Relocation and the resulting long-distance parenting happens for many different reasons, such as:

- A new or better job or business opportunity.
- A transfer or promotion within the current firm (which may or may not be truly optional).
- A new marriage or partnership with someone living in another location.
- An employment opportunity for a new partner.
- Moving closer to extended family for support.
- Wanting to make a fresh start away from the ex-partner.

A long-term or permanent move to a different state or even a new country is often harder on children than on their parents, especially when the parents are separated. Whether it is the resident parent who moves, taking the children with her and leaving their father as a long-distance parent, or the other parent who moves leaving his children, those children become long-distance children, and the relationship they have with their distant parent, already radically changed by the parents separating, will change again. Sometimes one or more children—often older teenagers—refuse to move with the parent they have always lived with, moving instead to live with the previously nonresident parent.

Long-distance moves inevitably disrupt contact between the

children and the nonresident parent. It is not only that many such moves involve enormous distances and therefore demanding and expensive travel for all future person-to-person contact, but also that despite the ease and ordinariness of tourist travel, crossing national or state borders, even nearby ones, brings separated parents and their parenting plans up against different legal systems and regulations.

Nonresident Parents Moving Farther Away from Children

If you want to move away from where your children live, either within the United States or abroad, you do not require permission or agreement from the resident parent, however much she wants you to stay in close contact with the children, and however

---

AMERICANS ON THE MOVE

According to the U.S. Census Bureau, out of a population of 282,556,000 people, 40,093,000 move each year. That's an overall percentage of 14.19 percent annually.

Of these 40-plus million people:

23,468,000 move within the same county.
7,728,000 move to a different county within the same state.
7,628,000 move to a different state.
1,269,000 move to a different country.

The number of moves vary by age; so does the distance moved.

The major new-move activity takes place among eighteen- to thirty-four-year-olds.

Couples with young children are the most likely to move a long distance.

If a move outside the same county is considered a "long-distance" move, there are 17 million annual long-distance moves, with more than a million of these moves outside the United States.

Source: David Bancroft Avrick, "How Many People Move Each Year—and Who Are They?," http://www.melissadata.com/enews/articles/0705b/1.htm

---

certain she feels that your relocation will work against that. Your move may go against the contact arrangements in the parenting plan you made with your ex and even against the advice of advisers, but unlike financial arrangements for maintenance, these are not legal commitments.

Resident Parents Taking Children to Live Elsewhere

Taking your children to live farther away from the nonresident parent is a very different matter from the nonresident parent moving farther away from the children. Many custody arrangements or parenting plans stipulate that the resident parent must consult the other parent before making any such move, and many nonresident parents refuse to countenance it.

Most of the "long-distance" moves parents make with their children are from one county or state to another. But helped by globalization and the boom in relationships between people from different parts of the world, an increasing number of separated parents are seeking to emigrate. Relocation to a new country, which is a positive move for many intact families, may be especially attractive to separated parents seeking a fresh start, but the number of international fights over child custody is going up.

Moving Away with Your Children

Most divorce agreements include residency clauses, which prevent the resident or custodial parent from taking the children to live beyond specified geographical limits. But even if you are the resident parent and subject to no such restriction, the children's other parent can object to any proposal to move the children farther away from his residence. If your proposed move is to another country, it is not up to the other parent to object but up to you to obtain his written consent. Do be aware of this, because if you move abroad without the consent of your ex, you will have abducted your children, which is, of course, a very serious crime.

TAKING CHILDREN TO LIVE IN A DIFFERENT STATE OR COUNTRY

Judith J. Wallerstein, a leading expert on divorce from Marin County, California, is quoted as saying that relocation "is the hottest issue in the divorce courts at the moment," and many other legal experts and social scientists say relocation cases, also known as move-aways, may be the most contentious and fastest-growing kind of custody litigation in the country today.

More nonresident parents—mostly fathers—are refusing to allow their children to move out of town (let alone out of state or country), forcing mothers—who about 80 percent of the time have physical custody of children—to remain in the same city. And more mothers are fighting back.

These cases are roiling families and courtrooms from California to Colorado to Connecticut. There are no reliable national statistics on these cases, but, as Leslie Eaton noted ten years ago: "the highest courts in at least seven states have tackled relocations in the last three years, and lawyers say they represent just the tip of the litigation iceberg."

When a disputed relocation case comes to court, the ruling must be made in line with "'the best interests of the child,' but there is little agreement about what that means. In many states, including New York, judges have a laundry list of factors to consider but no clear way to weigh their importance.... They [also] have to assess the motives for the proposed moves and for the objections. Does the parent who wants to move have a compelling reason, or is she just trying to keep the child away from the father? Does the parent who opposes the move really want to be involved with the child, or is he just trying to control his ex-wife?"

Source: Eaton 2004

- If the contact parent will not agree to your move, it will depend on permission from the court.
- If your application to the court is well prepared, it has a high chance of success though it may be frustratingly slow to be heard. It may be important for you to warn your future employer, landlord, or even partner of the length of time that is likely to elapse before you can travel.
- The court will need to be convinced that the move has been meticulously planned, is realistic, and would improve the

quality of life for the children. The court will want details of your job prospects or family contacts at your destination and will want to be assured that you have immediate accommodation and schooling (if relevant) in place. It will also take account of the wishes of any child who is considered old enough to give her point of view. If all that is in place, the court will tend toward granting your application.

- Some legal professionals believe that permission is sometimes given without due regard to the situation of the other parent and modern thinking on shared parenting. The court will satisfy itself that the proposed move abroad is not an attempt to exclude the other parent from the children's lives, and it will inquire what consideration you have given to the extra costs of visitation after the move, but that is all. The court's consideration of the welfare of the children and whether it is in their best interests to move abroad permanently give little weight to their loss of easy access to the other parent.

- The court will, however, try to ensure that visitation with the nonresident parent continues, although it will necessarily be more difficult and less frequent. If the court considers that once the move is made, visitation may not take place, it can add conditions—such as a surety or bond payment—to the permission to travel that is being given. If you then fail to cooperate with visits, the fund could support the travel or even the litigation costs of the contact parent. Realistically, though, unless you plan to relocate to a neighboring country, the costs of travel will often be prohibitive.

- If your planned new location is many hours of flying time away, travel costs are not the only bar to contact; distance and time may also be important. If at least one of the children is very young, good contact between the other parent and that child might have been established and maintained by frequent short visits—days or single overnights—and these will now be impossible (see chapter 7). Such a long journey will mean that only relatively long visits seem worthwhile, but even two or three such trips each year may take a visiting parent past his

---

LONG-DISTANCE PARENTING

"Fathering from afar may, however, become a skill, which current divorce rates make it imperative for men to learn. I was impressed to see Nelson Mandela talking to Arthur Miller on television, shortly after his release from twenty-seven years in jail, describing his efforts to father children he had barely known or touched, imparting guidance, boundaries, and love."

Source: Duffell 2000

---

leave entitlement and the option of children traveling to visit the parent will only be open to older teenagers and young adults.

Making the Best of Long-Distance Parenting

Like almost every situation in post-separation family life, the success of this one for children mostly depends on the relationship between their two parents. If the children live with you and your ex is at a distance, 50 percent of the responsibility for his continuing relationship with them belongs to you. It's even easier for you to alienate the children from a long-distance parent than from one who is close by and around every weekend, and even more important to be supportive.

The long-distance parent will have to work at staying in touch with the children using all the methods suggested earlier (see pp. 152–70). He is far more likely to succeed with your help than without it. For example, you need to help the children manage any time differences and understand when they can and cannot phone or make video calls. You need to help your ex set up a schedule for his calls and make sure the children are there for them.

It can be really difficult for a long-distance parent to get information about the children's lives. Share your own and anything you hear from schools, doctors, and any sports coaches or out-of-school teachers.

Look into online programs (some of them are developed especially for divorced parents) that allow you to provide information about the children that the long-distance parent can access at any time (and vice versa when the children visit him). Parents who have information tend to be more involved and feel more connected to their children.

Help keep the other parent "alive" for your children. Don't only allow them to display formal photos of the long-distance parent; also encourage two-way e-mailing of smartphone photos so they have immediate real-time pictures.

Do everything you can to make visits possible and enjoyable.

> **Divorced father of two boys, aged eight and eleven**
> "When I first heard that she was planning to go and work in Hong Kong, I didn't think she really would. Take the boys out of school, out of the state, away from me and their grandparents and all their friends? No way . . . But two weeks later she'd been offered the job; it was clear she was serious, and, well, I can honestly say I went into shock. After all the grief and work that went into settling things down after the divorce, I was going to lose them. She thought I might refuse my consent and drag the whole thing through court, but what was the point in making her hate me? It wouldn't have changed anything else in the end."

IF YOU ARE a long-distance parent because your ex has moved away with the children, you may be angry with her and sorry for yourself, but none of that will help the children. Remember that as the adult it is up to you to make and maintain contact with the children. Don't sit sadly by, hoping for a phone call or an e-mail. Call or send an e-mail yourself.

Don't be offended (or worse) if one of the children doesn't call back when you text or can't wait to get off the video call. These formal communications often interrupt children, who are busy with their lives, and then they can't think of anything to say. It helps if you avoid asking questions that have yes/no answers. "Did you have a good day?" may get you a yes or no and then silence. "What was the funniest thing that happened today?"

might get you a few words and even a giggle. Whichever way it goes, try to accept a quick call as the equivalent of a quick hug.

Set up a regular schedule for these contacts (especially if you are in separate time zones) and follow it as faithfully as you used to follow the schedule for contact visits. If you say you're going to call, call. If you are going to send an e-mail, do it. Your child needs to be able to count on you following through.

Conclusion

This book started with the importance of looking at family breakdown from the children's points of view, and it ends there, too. There are many books about divorce—this probably isn't the first one you have read—but most of them approach it as adults' business when it is very much children's business as well. I've been aware of this ever since my own family broke up when I was ten years old, but it's only now, after many years spent researching other aspects of child development and parenting, that turning around the way we handle family breakdown and its impact on children has come to seem both a priority and a possibility. It's a priority because more and more children are being affected, and it's a possibility because recent findings from attachment science show the way.

Right now only about half of all sixteen-year-olds are still living with both their parents, and the number of parents who separate while their children are under five is going up. Research over the last decade is showing us how damaging family breakdown is for children, but the way parental separation and divorce is handled is still as adult-centric as ever, and the current family law system is still adversarial, still focused on property and profit. Changes are urgently needed. By turning upside down what we now know about the harm parental separation does to children, we can begin to see what can be done to lessen it. Will that happen? Can parents who are separating face up to what that means to their children, and can divorce mediators, lawyers, and judges focus, and help their clients to focus, on what we now know to be children's essential needs?

PARENTS MATTER

The fundamental message of this book is that parents matter even more than we knew—and in unexpected ways. That still-growing body of research into brain development offers today's mothers and fathers a new understanding of their own and each other's importance. This is the first generation of parents in a position to realize that from birth, or even before, a child's attachment, first to the mother (or her substitute) and soon also to the father, is responsible not only for his health and happiness today—which is obvious—but also for his entire growth and development as a person, brain and body, now and forever, which is not obvious at all.

MOTHERS MATTER MOST AT FIRST

Everything that happens in people's development depends on what happened before, so whatever the age of a child you are concerned for, new knowledge of infancy, the starting point, is vital. Five-sixths of a baby's brain grows after birth and does so astonishingly fast, more than doubling in size in the first year with forty thousand new synapses (connections) forming every second. Only in this generation have we learned that this brain growth is not just a matter of maturation and genetics. The way each individual baby's brain grows and weaves itself together and functions largely depends on his experiences in the last pre-natal months and the first year or two after birth.

Significant experiences begin to impinge on that development while a baby is still in his mother's womb, which is why she is uniquely important to him. And even once he is delivered, his early experiences continue to center on his mother, if she is available, or whoever stands in for her, if she is not, so the emotional relationship he shares and builds with her is the foundation of all that is to follow: the actual structure and functioning of his brain, his personality, the way he will manage his feelings and relationships and cope with stress throughout his life.

At birth, the left-hand "thinking" part of a baby's brain has yet to develop. His right-brain (and newly separated body) experiences and reacts to deep, primitive feelings: to fear and anger, to excitement and joy, but because he himself does not have the brain capacity to regulate those potentially overwhelming feelings, he relies on his primary attachment figure to lend him the use of her brain to keep his feelings in balance and bring him back from terror or excitement to calm.

A baby's primary attachment figure can, of course, be his father, but it will usually be his mother, not only because her relationship with the baby got a head start while he was inside her but also because most (though not all) females are better than most (but not all) males at right-brain responsiveness. A mother who is attuned to her baby responds to his right brain with her own. When he cries, she does not need to use her adult, developed left brain to think about what she has heard or plan what she will do about it; she simply responds, often leaving the TV and starting up the stairs before she is conscious of having heard that cry. She and her baby communicate without words or conscious thought, using facial expressions, different emotionally loaded tones of voice (including "motherese"), and a lot of touching, gesturing, and hugging.

All this baby stuff that used to be taken as much for granted as petting a puppy, and even rationed for fear of "spoiling," is now known to be enormously important to a child's development. A baby's right brain cannot grow and develop fully without these intimate human experiences. They are what get imprinted into his brain's circuits. And how a parent provides those experiences for him largely depends on the emotional experiences that were imprinted and stored in the circuits of *her* right brain when she was an infant with *her* mother. These nonverbal communication skills that we learn in infancy are used throughout our lives in all our interpersonal and intimate relationships, including romantic or marital partnerships. And their patterns tend to repeat across generations. Family breakdown often contributes to disturbed childhood attachment, but childhood attachment stressors also play a big part in divorce and the custody battles that so often follow.

FATHERS SOON MATTER JUST AS MUCH

It is because a baby's primary attachment starts in the womb and is therefore almost always to his mother that accounts of infant development tend to imply that the mother is the primary parent and the father secondary. That is a misreading of the facts. A child's relationship with each parent is equally important but different both in timing and in kind. In the right-brain-dominated first year, what babies need most is maternal regulation of otherwise uncontrollable emotions: soothing and reassurance. But as long as the father is sufficiently available, the baby will be gradually building an attachment to him also that will intensify in the second year, when the left brain enters a growth spurt. Now exploration and understanding of the physical world come to the fore, supported by new experiences and challenges provided by fathers' attention and play.

People go on developing attachments all through their lives—to other family members; to adults from outside the family such as teachers; to childhood and adolescent "best friends"; and eventually to adult sexual partners—but these first attachments are the foundation of all that follow.

PARENTAL SEPARATION IS WORSE FOR THE CHILDREN

Fresh understanding of the full extent of both parents' importance to their children throws the significance of family breakdown into sharp relief. Parental separation or divorce is very seldom pain-free for anyone, but it is clear now that because relationships with parents are central to children's lifelong development it is most damaging to them. Furthermore, no child is too young or too old to be affected by it. Whether the offspring of separating parents is six months or six, sixteen, or twenty-six years old, having the family split up and mother and father living separately from each other and interacting with her only one at a time will always be emotionally as well as practically disruptive, miserable, bewildering, and sad.

Parents sometimes assume that babies who are too young to understand what is going on are too young to be damaged by it, but a baby's relationship with that "primary caregiver" (usually, though not always, mom) is the most important aspect of his world, and anything that upsets or distracts her will impinge on him, even before he is born. At the other end of childhood, parents often congratulate themselves on delaying a long-planned separation until the children are old enough to "understand." But they are not entitled to do so. What those adult children are likely to take from that separation is that their personal history was built on lies and that their childhood memories and sense of identity are false.

These are not messages parents, grandparents, or step-parents-in-the-making want to hear, so people don't talk much about the effects on children of parents separating. Considering that about half of all children live through and with family breakdown, it's astonishing how little it is acknowledged. If half the children in your child's school year faced a physical disaster, such as losing a limb, everyone would be talking about it all the time. As it is, though, when discussion does take place, it usually stresses how resilient children are and how quickly they'll get over it. Unfortunately, that's wishful thinking. Children are not born resilient (though they will become more so if their attachments in the first years are secure), and their parents' parting is too basic a fracture in their social and emotional development for them to "get over it" in the sense of putting it behind them and getting on with life as it would have been. Children adapt to new circumstances and relationships—what choice do they have?—but even when they seem to have healed there will be scars remaining.

Despite the efforts of some individuals, the current adversarial family law system does little to help separating parents protect their children. The way courts deal with separation, divorce, and custody sometimes even encourages parents to fight with each other and to make outrageous claims about each other's behavior, instead of encouraging reconciliation and ensuring that children's needs are met in practice as well as in theory. And although most parents at first intend to protect their children from adult fallout, many become so submerged in their own disrupted lives, their anger and hurt, that they may unwittingly unleash in their offspring a lifetime of upset, misplaced guilt, and conflicted loyalty.

It should be understood that these pages do not aim to suggest that because family breakdown is so bad parents should stay together for the sake of the children. An unhappy partnership held together only by responsibility is unlikely to last for long in our current "me-culture," where personal fulfillment is almost a duty, and is unlikely to make for good parenting or happy children in the meantime. Vague long-term dissatisfaction isn't as obvious as open parental irritation or depression, or the sexual unfaithfulness, arguments, enmity, and especially violence that poison many children's growing up, but if the long-term relationship between parents has become joyless or intolerable to one or both of them, it will be a chilly environment for their children today and will model loveless relationships for them as they grow up.

PUTTING CHILDREN FIRST

We have to accept separation and divorce as a counterbalance to failed cohabitation and marriage. Contemporary society, where many people live into their eighties, cannot manage without such a relationship safety valve. But the well-being of the children who will grow up to form that society in their turn is being put at unnecessary risk by the way that safety valve is deployed. It is clear that it could be managed better. Instead of asking "Should people stay together for the children's sake?," we should be asking "Can women and men who cannot live in peaceful comfort together be better mothers and fathers when they are apart?" The question is rarely asked, because who gets divorced in order to be a better parent? And if it was asked, the answer would be assumed to be no. But it is clear that when separating adults can make the needs of their children their priority the answer may often be yes.

Almost everyone pays lip service to the notion of putting children first, but actually doing it is not something everybody takes for granted. Some parents ask why children's happiness should come first: Is their own happiness not just as important? The simple answer is that people who are parents may divorce or leave each other but cannot divorce and should not ever leave their children, not only because children's current happiness and well-being depends on them but also because children's development into the adults of the future is at stake. If we want to be really me-me-me about it, we should think about how those children will care for us when *we* are dependent on *them*.

MAKING THE BEST OF A BAD JOB

There's no escaping the fact that family breakdown is always a bad break for everyone, but the message of this book is not all doom and gloom. If we are aware of, understand, and learn from the same growing body of research that shows how damaging it can be, we can make the best of that bad job for children.

A vital first step is to reverse the adult-centric way parental separation is dealt with, not only in families but often in law-yers' offices and family courts, too. When a family breaks down, everyone's energy goes into fighting for or trying to reconcile the interests of father and mother. An important and often-ignored fact coming out of that research is that children's interests may be entirely different.

TREATING CHILDREN AS PEOPLE RATHER THAN POSSESSIONS

Parental separation means a lot of sharing and dividing up of property, and in the name of "equal parenting" some children are shared between parents like the DVD collection. But children are not chattels. Contact or custody arrangements that seem "fair" to the parent or the court may be not just "unfair" but damagingly wrong for a child. In the long run, fathers are as important as mothers, and many studies now show that children, adolescents, and adults who have close relationships with their fathers do better everywhere and forever—at school, at work, and in their social lives—than those who do not, so it is clearly highly desir-able that children of all ages have the best possible relationship with both parents. But what about the short run? When a law-yer bids for his client to have the baby son he has never before looked after alone live with him on weekends, they may both be ignoring clear evidence that such sudden overnight separations from the mother are not only usually distressing but also poten-tially damaging to the secure attachment and even therefore the brain development of any baby or toddler. And when people say that it's "only fair" for a father and mother to care for their five-year-old daughter on alternate weeks, they mean that it is fair to the adults, not that they think it's the best possible parenting plan for the child. These arrangements sometimes seem to be made by people who are seeing a child as a possession and her presence as their right, rather than seeing her as a person, with individual needs.

MUTUAL PARENTING

The final lessons these same research data can teach go full circle back to our new understanding of the overwhelming importance to children of their relationships with parents. They tell us that when marriage or partnership has definitely ended what matters most to children of any age is that parenting has not. When relationships between wives and husbands fail, children's relationships with mothers and fathers must at all costs be protected and maintained. Those costs can be high (outside as well as inside a lawyer's office) because, as the many children's voices in this book make clear, the needs and wants of a particular child may be completely different from the needs and wants of her father or her mother, and it is the child, with her whole future development as a person ahead of her, who must come first.

It is difficult for anyone who has not been in that position to imagine what it costs a father who loves his child but hasn't spent much time with her to acknowledge that if he and his partner cannot live together, living with the mother is probably better for that baby right now than living with him. And it is equally difficult to imagine the cost to a mother who, while bruised by betrayal and furious with her ex, must nevertheless welcome and act on the fact that the children still love and need their daddy.

When a family breaks down, what matters most to children of all ages is not their parents' physical separation but their enmity. The separated parents who do their children most damage are those who fight over them and try to alienate them from the other parent; such parenting is broken. Children survive family breakdown better if parents can confine their adult issues, anger, and bitterness to their man-woman relationship, so that their relationship as mother and father can remain polite. But what will best ease the children through their inevitable misery when the family unit is broken is for separated partners to muster selfless concern for the children. That selfless concern can keep them united in their determination to carry on being, and helping each other to be, loving parents. I have called that mutual parenting, and it is the best possible way forward from family breakdown. No longer a wife, husband, or partner but always and forever a mother or father.

Acknowledgments

When Parents Part was not an obvious or an easy book to write.

Parental separation and divorce figure in the experience of more than half of American couples, and there are many books out there written to help them. Why write another?

The topic floated around in my head for several years while I was busy with other research. New findings on the importance of children's relationships with parents were being published; I talked to children and young people whose families had split up; gradually an answer to that question took shape. Another book was needed, but a book written from children's point of view: not primarily aimed at helping separating parents but at helping them to minimize the impact on children, from infancy to adulthood, and to find ways to go on being their fathers and mothers when they were no longer husbands and wives.

It is not an easy subject, but Katherine Hourigan, my editor since 1974, and my friend of thirty-five years, was determined to publish it. I have never brought out a book in the United States that Kathy did *not* edit, and this one certainly would not have happened without her. I am, as always, proud to be on Knopf's list, and am grateful, of course, to Sonny Mehta, and to Christine Gillespie, Diana Secker Tesdale, and Erinn McGrath for their help.

Putting together a book that incorporates so many voices is complicated, so I owe a particular thank-you to Ellen Feldman, who is the book's production editor, and to Cassandra Pappas, its designer. If *When Parents Part* says what I meant it to say and looks good, it is because of them (if not, it's because of me!).

References

American Psychological Association. 2013. *The Changing Role of the Modern Day Father*. Available at http://apa.org/pi/families/resources/changing-father.aspx.

Brown, A., and J. M. Jones. 2012. "Separation, Divorce Linked to Sharply Lower Wellbeing." Available at http://www.gallup.com/poll/154001/separation-divorce-linked-sharply-lower-wellbeing.aspx.

Casey, B. J., R. M. Jones, and T. A. Hare. 2008. "The Adolescent Brain." *Annals of the New York Academy of Sciences* 1124:111–26.

Cheadle, J. E., P. R. Amato, and V. King. 2010. "Patterns of Nonresidential Father Contact." *Demography* 47 (1): 205–25.

Clark, Charles S. 1996. "Is It Time to Crack Down on Easy Divorces?" *Marriage and Divorce: CQ Researcher* 6 (May 10): 409–32.

Copen, C. E., K. Daniels, J. Vespa, and W. D. Mosher. 2012. *First Marriages in the United States: Data from the 2006–2010 National Survey of Family Growth*. National Health Statistics Report no. 29 (March 22). Available at http://www.cdc.gov/nchs/data/nhsr/nhsr049.pdf.

Crittenden, P. M., and A. H. Claussen. 2000. *The Organization of Attachment Relationships: Maturation, Culture, and Context*. New York: Cambridge University Press.

Deblaquiere, J., L. Moloney, and R. Weston. 2012. "Parental Separation and Grandchildren: The Multiple Perspectives of Grandparents." *Family Matters* 90:68–76.

DiFonzo, J. H. 2011. "How Marriage Became Optional: Cohabitation, Gender, and the Emerging Functional Norms." *Rutgers Journal of Law & Public Policy* 8 (3): 521–66.

Duffell, N. 2000. *The Making of Them: The British Attitude to Children and the Boarding School System*. London: Lone Arrow Press.

Eaton, Leslie. 2004. "Divorced Parents Move, and Custody Gets Trickier." *New York Times*. August 8. Available at http://www.nytimes.com/2004/08/08/nyregion/divorced-parents-move-and-custody-gets-trickier.html.

Fuller-Thompson, E. 2000. "American Grandparents Providing Extensive

Child Care to Their Grandchildren: Prevalence and Profile." *The Gerontologist* 41 (2): 201–9.

Gillett, J. 2005. "I'm Leaving on a Jet Plane, Don't Know When I'll Be Back Again: Can I Take the Kids with Me?" *Family Law Journal.* Available at www.familylawweek.co.uk.

Hanushek, E. A., J. F. Kain, and S. G. Rivkin. 2004. "Disruption Versus Tiebout Improvement: The Costs and Benefits of Switching Schools." *Journal of Public Economics* 88:1721–46.

Jost, Kenneth, and Marilyn Robinson. 1991. "What Can Be Done to Help Children of Divorce?" Children and Divorce. *CQ Researcher* 1 (June 7). Available at https://suite.io/cathy-herold/530x2jm.

Judiciary of England and Wales. 2012. *Annual Report of the Office of the Head of International Family Justice for England and Wales.* Available at http://www.judiciary.gov.uk/wp-content/uploads/JCO/Documents/Reports/international_family_justice_2013.pdf.

The King's Fund. 2012. *British Social Attitudes Survey 2012: Public Satisfaction with the NHS and Its Services.* Available at http://www.kingsfund.org.uk/projects/bsa-survey-2012.

Kirby, J. 2012. "Single Parent Families and Poverty in the US." Master's thesis, Ohio State University. Available at www3.uakron.edu/schulze/401/readings/singleparfam.htm.

Kirkland Weir, I. 2009. *When Did You Last See Your Father?* Talk to Hertfordshire Family Forum, November 26. Available at http://www.neves-solicitors.co.uk/site/library/privategeneral/WhenDidYouLastSeeYourFather.html.

Lagattuta, K. H., L. Sayfan, and C. Bamford. 2012. "Do You Know How I Feel? Parents Underestimate Worry and Overestimate Optimism Compared to Child Self-Report." *Journal of Experimental Child Psychology* 13 (2): 211–32.

Leach, P. 1994. *Children First.* New York: Vintage.

———. 2010a. *Child Care Today.* New York: Vintage.

———. 2010b. *Your Baby & Child from Birth to Age Five.* New York: Knopf.

Lewis, C., and M. E. Lamb. 2007. *Understanding Fatherhood: A Review of Recent Research.* London: Joseph Rowntree Foundation.

Luo, Y., T. A. LaPierre, M. E. Hughes, and L. J. Waite. 2012. "Grandparents Providing Care to Grandchildren: A Population-Based Study of Continuity and Change." *Journal of Family Issues* 33 (9): 1143–67.

McIntosh, J. E. 2011. "Special Considerations for Infants and Toddlers in Separation/Divorce: Developmental Issues in the Family Law Context." Available at http://www.child-encyclopedia.com/divorce-and-separation/according-experts/special-considerations-infants-and-toddlers.

———. 2012. "Infants and Overnights: The Drama, the Players and Their Scripts." Plenary Paper, Association of Family and Conciliation Courts 49th Annual Conference, Chicago.

McIntosh, J. E., M. K. Pruett, and J. B. Kelly. 2014. "Parental Separation and Overnight Care of Young Children, Part II: Putting Theory into Practice." *Family Court Review* 52 (2): 256–62.

McIntosh, J. E., B. Smyth, M. Kelaher, Y. Wells, and C. Long. 2010. *Post-separation Parenting Arrangements and Developmental Outcomes for Infants and Children.* Collected Reports for the Australian Government Attorney General's Department.

Metsä-Simola, N., and P. Martikainen. 2013a. "Divorce and Changes in the Prevalence of Psychotropic Medication Use: A Register-Based Longitudinal Study Among Middle-Aged Finns." *Social Science & Medicine* 94:71–80.

———. 2013b. "The Short-Term and Long-Term Effects of Divorce on Mortality Risk in a Large Finnish Cohort, 1990–2003." *Population Studies (Camb)* 67 (1): 97–110.

Millward, C. 1998. *Family Relationship and Intergenerational Exchange in Later Life.* Working paper no. 15. Melbourne: Australian Institute of Family Studies.

Mindful Policy Group. 2014. *The Pledge for Children.* Available at http://www.mindfulpolicygroup.com/policy-areas/the-pledge-for-children/.

Nielsen, L., W. V. Fabticius, E. Kruk, and R. E. Emery. 2012. "Shared Parenting: Facts & Fiction." Timeless Attachments: Research and Policy Implications. Workshop 26, Association of Family and Conciliation Courts 49th Annual Conference, Chicago.

Office for National Statistics. 2014. *Marriages, Cohabitations, Civil Partnerships and Divorces.* Available at http://www.ons.gov.uk/ons/taxonomy/index.html?nscl = Marriages%2C + Cohabitations%2C%20 + Civil + Partnerships + and + Divorces.

Office of the Head of International Family Justice, Lord Justice Thorpe. 2012. *Taking Children to Live Abroad.*

Pruett, M. K., J. E. McIntosh, and J. B. Kelly. 2014. "Parental Separation and Overnight Care of Young Children, Part I: Consensus Through Theoretical and Empirical Integration." *Family Court Review* 52 (2): 240–55.

Rodda, M., J. Hallgarten, and J. Freeman. 2013. *Between the Cracks: Exploring In-Year Admissions in Schools in England.* Available at http://www.thersa.org/__data/assets/pdf_file/0007/1527316/RSA_Education_Between_the_cracks_report.pdf.

Schore, A. N. 2012. *The Science of the Art of Psychotherapy.* New York: W. W. Norton.

———. 2014. "Early Interpersonal Neurobiological Assessment of Attachment and Autistic Spectrum Disorders." *Frontiers in Psychology.* September 23.

Schore, A. N., and J. McIntosh. 2011. "Attachment Theory and the Emotional Revolution in Neuroscience." *Family Court Review* 49 (3): 501–12.

Solomon, J., and C. George. 1999. "The Place of Disorganization in Attachment Theory: Linking Classic Observations with Contemporary Findings." In J. Solomon and C. George, eds., *Attachment Disorganization.* New York: Guilford Press.

Thompson, H. 2011. *Home Alone.* Available at http://yougov.co.uk/news/2011/02/17/homealone/.

United Nations Economic Commission for Europe. 2014. *Statistics.* Available at: http://www.unece.org/stats/.

Wames, T., and M. Crane. 2004. *Homelessness in the Over-Fifties.* Report by the Economic and Social Research Council.

Weissmann, Jordan. 2014. "For Millennials, Out-of-Wedlock Childbirth Is the Norm: So Now What?" *Slate.* June 23. Available at http://www.slate.com/articles/business/moneybox/2014/06/for_millennials_out_of_wedlock_childbirth_is_the_norm_now_what.html.

Young Children in Divorce and Separation (YCIDS). Online program: Children Beyond Dispute. Available at http://www.familytransitions.com.au/Family_Transitions/Parent_Resources.html.

Index

12-19
d